GUITAR *signature licks*

Audio Access Included

MW01039840

DREAM THEATER

by Troy Stetina

PLAYBACK+
Speed • Pitch • Balance • Loop

To access audio visit:
www.halleonard.com/mylibrary

Enter Code
3475-2044-8456-2113

Cover photo: John Zocco

ISBN 978-1-4768-8945-0

HAL•LEONARD®

7777 W. BLUEMOUND RD. P.O. BOX 13819 MILWAUKEE, WI 53213

In Australia Contact:
Hal Leonard Australia Pty. Ltd.
4 Lentara Court
Cheltenham, Victoria, 3192 Australia
Email: ausadmin@halleonard.com.au

Visit Hal Leonard Online at
www.halleonard.com

CONTENTS

PAGE   TITLE

INTRODUCTION

Dream Theater is the world's preeminent progressive metal/rock art band, known for precise execution, virtuosic performance, philosophical and thoughtful lyrics, odd meters, and non-formulaic song structures. In short, Dream Theater is a band of musician's musicians: the nexus of a relentless pursuit of technical heavy-music mastery with uncompromising artistic vision. This style came about as the result of a synthesis of the progressive rock of Rush, Yes, and Pink Floyd with the heavy metal of Iron Maiden plus a dose of speed metal and glam metal elements—metal with melody and art rock roots. While characteristic distorted metal guitar tones drive the band sonically, the song structures are extremely complex, at times perhaps even bordering on indulgent. The focus is on technical precision and flawless execution rather than the repetitive, heavy riffing characteristic of standard metal.

Guitarist John Peter Petrucci was born July 12, 1967 and grew up in Kings Park, New York, on Long Island. He began playing guitar at age 12 and quickly became consumed by his passion for it, practicing six hours a day or more to hone his technical abilities. His early influences included Steve Morse, Al Di Meola, Steve Howe, Allan Holdsworth, Stevie Ray Vaughan, Randy Rhoads, Joe Satriani, Steve Vai, Alex Lifeson, Yngwie Malmsteen, Rush, Yes, Iron Maiden, Metallica, the Dixie Dregs, and more. To further his musical ambitions, after high school John attended the Berklee College of Music in Boston, Massachusetts, along with schoolmate and bassist John Myung. There they met drummer Mike Portnoy, and the creative nucleus that would become Dream Theater was born.

In 1985, the trio first named themselves "Majesty" and could be heard covering Rush and Iron Maiden songs in the school's rehearsal rooms. John then asked his high school band mate Kevin Moore to cover keyboards, and another friend from Long Island, Chris Collins, was brought in as vocalist. Shortly after this, Portnoy, Myung, and Petrucci decided to abandon their studies at Berklee in order to focus more on the band, as they had begun performing shows in the New York City area and were spending a great deal of time developing original music.

All was not going well within the lineup, however, and after several months Chris Collins was fired. It was late 1986, and the search for a new vocalist went on for nearly a full year, until Charlie Dominici came on board. With their new singer and more shows, the band began to gain significant visibility in the New York City area. An unexpected result of this was that a Las Vegas group named Majesty also became aware of them and threatened legal action for infringement for the use of the name. A name change was deemed appropriate; Mike Portnoy's father suggested "Dream Theater"—the name of a small theater in Monterey, California—and it stuck.

The first record deal was achieved with Mechanic Records, a division of MCA, in June of 1988, and the band began recording their debut album shortly thereafter. With hopes riding high, tracking was completed in just ten days, and the album, *When Dream and Day Unite*, was completed in three weeks. However, when it was released in 1989 to less interest than the initial demos had garnered, and the label failed to deliver on their promised level of support, the band was greatly disappointed and financially restricted to performing locally. Only five concerts materialized for the first "tour." It was a disappointing start, but the determined musicians pressed on.

At this time, the band was also increasingly unhappy with the vocal limitations of Dominici, as his decidedly pop vocal stylings were at growing odds with the band's progressive direction. Portnoy is reported to have said, "It was like having Billy Joel singing in Queensrÿche." It just wasn't working. As Dominici departed on good terms, the band fought to be released from contract with Mechanic and began writing new material—material that would eventually become *Images and Words*. It would take longer than anyone would have guessed to find the right front man. The band auditioned over 200 singers in the two-year period that followed before finally settling on Canadian vocalist James LaBrie in January, 1991. But when it was right, things fell into place, and on the strength of a three-song demo, Dream Theater was signed to Atco Records, a division of Elektra. (This was later made available as *The Atco Demos* via the Dream Theater fan club.)

The first album recorded under the Atco label, *Images and Words* (1992), included "Another Day," the song chosen to be the album's promotional single and video, but it made little commercial impact. The song "Pull Me Under," however, turned out to be a surprise success, gathering a large amount of radio airplay with no organized promotion by the band or the label. In response, Atco also produced a video clip for that song, which found a receptive audience on MTV, received heavy rotation, and introduced Dream Theater to a much wider audience.

Capitalizing on this success, the band also began relentless touring in the US and Japan, pushing *Images and Words* to achieve gold certification in the US and platinum in Japan. Dream Theater was now "on the map" and positioned to become a major voice to define heavy progressive music. And they succeeded at this brilliantly. By 2012, the band had sold over 12 million records worldwide, and *Metropolis, Pt. 2: Scenes from a Memory* (1999) was ranked as the number one all-time progressive album by Rolling Stone magazine. Dream Theater has achieved commercial success on its own terms in a genre that unyieldingly eschews the mainstream taste.

Stylistically, John Petrucci is perhaps best known for his lightning-fast alternate picking with clean synchronization between the left and right hands. Far from overusing his speed to the point of redundancy, however, John applies his skills tastefully and in a balanced way; his intense shredding technique is often intertwined with evocative, slow moving lines. A mature sense of composition is clearly in the navigation seat here, and this gives his soloing forays a deeper sense of purpose. Contrast and momentum, flavor and spice, as well as energy and effected textures figure prominently in the artist's toolbag.

This makes total sense when one considers the larger perspective—John Petrucci is more than a guitarist; rather he is a musician and composer who happens to play the guitar. That is to say, his vision extends far beyond the "guitar part" per se. As a composer, he often contributes vocal melodies—his baritone vocals can be heard on several demo versions of songs—and as a singer he has performed backing vocals since the *Awake* tour (1994). In addition, he has been an active lyrical contributor, writing several songs on every Dream Theater album. He has also been in the production seat since 1999, so it is no surprise that John brings a level of compositional finesse to his guitar work. It is simply an extension of composition.

In the following pages, join me as we investigate a number of John's trademark guitar moments and uncover just what it is that has made this remarkable guitarist at the heart of this remarkable band so successful and riveting to a generation of musicians.

EQUIPMENT

Dream Theater guitarist John Petrucci has employed a number of different guitar effects in quite complex switching rigs over the years. However, his amp choice has been Mesa Boogie in one form or another from 1994 to present. (For *Images and Words*, he used a Marshall JMP-1.) Specifically, on the *Awake* album in 1994, Petrucci used a combination of Mesa Boogie Dual Rectifier and Mark IIC+ amps, preferring to track two slightly different tones to create a fuller overall sound. For albums that followed, he has generally continued this practice of using multiple amps, including the Dual Rectifier, Mark IIC+, Mark IV, TriAxis, Formula, Road King Series 1, Lone Star, Mark V, 2:90 power amp, and Royal Atlantic RA-100. For a specific enumeration of which amps were used on which albums and tours, you can visit *en.wikipedia.org/wiki/John_Petrucci*.

For a detailed visual depiction of his guitar rig as it consisted in 2002 during the *Six Degrees of Inner Turbulence* tour, see *www.guitargeek.com/john-petrucci-dream-theater-guitar-rig-and-gear-setup-2002*. The signal flow chart shown there is the result of an interview by GuitarGeek.com with John and his guitar tech and gives a good insight into how such a complex rig actually works.

More recently, John's complete rig for the recent *A Dramatic Turn of Events* (2011) tour, which began in 2011 and continued until September, 2012, was as follows:

ELECTRIC GUITARS

Music Man John Petrucci Signature Models with DiMarzio Signature Crunch Lab Bridge Pickups and DiMarzio Signature LiquiFire Neck Pickups

JPXi 6 (three in standard tuning)

JPXi 7-String (standard tuning with low B)

JP BFR 7-String Koa Top (standard tuning with low B)

JPXi Silver Burst 6 (standard tuning down a whole step)

JPXi 6 (standard tuning down two whole steps)

JPXi 6 (standard tuning down a half step)

JP BFR Tobacco Burst Baritone (A tuning)

ACOUSTIC GUITAR

Taylor 30th Anniversary Acoustic Guitar

PEDALBOARD

Axess Electronics FX-1 Midi Controller

Ernie Ball 25K Stereo Volume Pedal

Dunlop Crybaby Remote Pedal

Boss TU-3 Tuner

Dunlop Crybaby Remote Pedal for Center Stage

Custom Steel Diamond Plate Foot Rests with ButtKicker Drivers installed for that ultimate thump!

AMPS AND EFFECTS

Mesa Boogie Mark V heads

Fractal Audio Axe FX 2 Guitar Preamp and Effects Processor

Framptone A/B Box

Dunlop DCR-2SR Crybaby Rack Module

Keeley Mod TS9DX Flexi-4X2 (Tube Screamer Mod)

Analog Man King of Tone Overdrive

Analog Man TS808 (Tube Screamer Mod)

Boss PH-3 Phaser

MXR EVH Flanger

Carl Martin Compressor

Axess Electronics Switchers

Mark Snyder Custom Interface/ Switcher

Furman AR Pro Power Conditioner

Mesa Boogie Traditional Rectifier 4X12 Cabinets with Celestion Vintage 30 speakers

ACCESSORIES

Jim Dunlop JP Shield Black Jazz III Picks

Mogami Cables

Neutrik Connectors

DiMarzio Black Cliplock Guitar Straps

Sensaphonics 2 XS In-Ear Monitors

Ernie Ball RPS Strings

John uses .10 gauge strings (Ernie Ball RPS Regular Slinky) when playing in standard tuning. However, for the various slack tunings, he likes to increase the gauge to heavier strings, with the goal being to approximate the same string tension for the slack tunings as the .10 gauge has in standard tuning. In other words, the lower the tuning, the heavier the string gauges used.

DISCOGRAPHY

The songs in this volume can be found on the following albums:

"Pull Me Under" – *Images and Words* (1992)

"Under a Glass Moon" – *Images and Words* (1992)

"Erotomania" – *Awake* (1994)

"Fatal Tragedy" – *Metropolis, Pt. 2: Scenes from a Memory* (1999)

"Home" – *Metropolis, Pt. 2: Scenes from a Memory* (1999)

"The Glass Prison" – *Six Degrees of Inner Turbulence* (2002)

"Endless Sacrifice" – *Train of Thought* (2003)

"In the Presence of Enemies, Pt. 1" – *Systematic Chaos* (2007)

"The Count of Tuscany" – *Black Clouds & Silver Linings* (2009)

"On the Backs of Angels" – *A Dramatic Turn of Events* (2011)

"Breaking All Illusions" – *A Dramatic Turn of Events* (2011)

"Behind the Veil" – *Dream Theater* (2013)

ABOUT THE AUDIO

To access the audio examples that accompany this book, simply go to **www.halleonard.com/mylibrary** and enter the code found on page 1. Each music figure in the book includes a full-band audio demo, and for the more difficult passages, a slow demo of the isolated guitar is provided.

Guitar: Jordan Baker

Bass: Jordan Baker

Drums: Chris Romero

Keyboards: Chris Romero

Recorded, mixed, and mastered by Jordan Baker and Chris Romero

ABOUT THE AUTHOR

Troy Stetina is a guitarist and music educator specializing in rock, metal, and shred guitar. He has authored over 40 book/audio and DVD guitar methods, including *Speed Mechanics for Lead Guitar*, which has guided a generation of players toward guitar mastery. Troy endorses PRS Guitars, the Troy Stetina Custom Signature Guitar by Dimis, Engl amps, and Dunlop strings and picks. For workshop dates, advanced lessons, and tips, visit Troy on the web at *www.stetina.com*.

PULL ME UNDER

(*Images and Words*, 1992)

Words and Music by Kevin LaBrie, Kevin Moore, John Myung, John Petrucci and Michael Portnoy

"Pull Me Under" is widely considered to be Dream Theater's signature song. Whether or not this is true, it certainly was the breakthrough song that launched the band into public awareness with radio airplay and extensive MTV video rotation. Yet to the band, which has always sought to keep a certain defining distance from the mainstream, it was just another song and a complete accident that it caught widespread public attention. Drummer Mike Portnoy summed it up in a radio interview, saying, "...it was just an eight and a half minute song, and it was just a fluke for MTV and radio play to happen."

The label capitalized on the interest and released it as a promotional single, which peaked at number 10 on the *Billboard* Mainstream Rock Chart. And while a handful of other Dream Theater singles would also appear on the charts over the years, "Pull Me Under" would be the only single to actually make it into the Top 10. Never given to missing an opportunity for lighthearted fun, it was this fact to which the band ironically alluded in their titling of the 2008 compilation album *Dream Theater's Greatest Hit (...and 21 Other Pretty Cool Songs)*. For a band clearly not striving to create "hits," it cannot be argued that "Pull Me Under" has created a legacy and remains the band's most widely recognized song. It is still performed on world tours, and live versions appear on the recordings *Live at the Marquee*, *Once in a LIVEtime*, *Live at Budokan*, as well as the DVD release, *Images and Words: Live in Tokyo*. It is also a playable master track in the *Guitar Hero World Tour (Guitar Hero IV)* game.

Figure 1—Intro, Verse

The opening gradually builds with clean guitar in a repeating four-measure phrase until it kicks in at 1:15 with a grinding metal riff. This utilizes the same harmonic content as the opening (not shown here), but now in the form of an E pedal tone riff with a 16th "reverse gallop" rhythmic figure motif leading each measure. Specifically, the moving chords on beat 2 recall the same A–G, F#–G, C#–G motion first established in the opening, except here in the riff, John is interpreting the notes as 5th dyads in standard metal fashion and further calls upon the tritone motion of C# to G for added melodic tension. Finally, the B5, C5, and D5 chords in measure 4 are inverted (the 5th is sounded below the root) for a thicker texture giving a hint toward the darker metal styles. And this is even further reinforced by swapping F5 (borrowed from the E Phrygian mode) in place of D5 on the repeat.

The riff next evolves rhythmically with the addition of upbeat accent points on both the "ands" of beats 3 and 4 in each measure as the keyboard enters. This acts to build the tension and energy further until dropping off suddenly at measure 11 with the interlocking guitar rhythm and snare. This is an "idling" moment and sets up a new groove for the verse to follow. As the E5 chord is palm-muted on the doubled 16ths, be careful to damp the strings with your fretting hand to stop their sustain and produce clean rests on each upbeat.

At the verse, the doubled-16th rhythmic motif is continued, but now with a palm-muted E pedal tone filling out where the rests were, while the chords on the downbeats evolve into tense dissonances. First, we see Esus2, formed in this case by two stacked 5th intervals, E–B–F# (low to high). The next chord is formed by simply raising each note of Esus2 up one scale tone of the E minor scale, giving us the notes F#–C–G (low to high). Rising scalarly in this fashion maintains the same dissonant texture, albeit one chord higher in this "harmonized 5th" approach. The third measure is Esus4, another dissonance, this time in the form of stacked 4th intervals. The phrase concludes with

C5 power chords and then the dissonant C(♭5) shape. The next time around on this four-measure sequence, the pattern ends with F rather than C, recalling the preceding riff's ending sequence and nicely tying things together compositionally.

Fig. 1

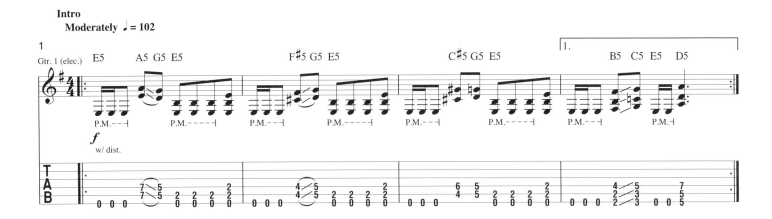

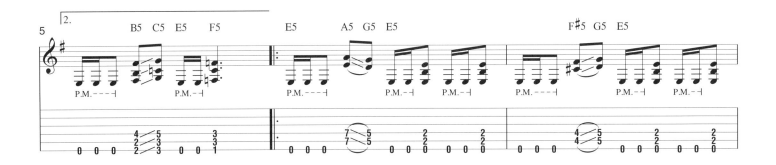

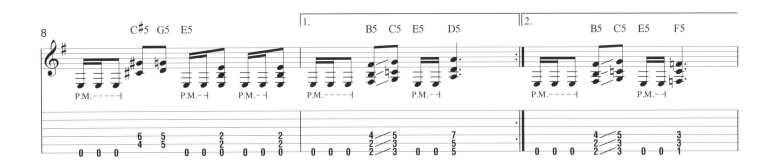

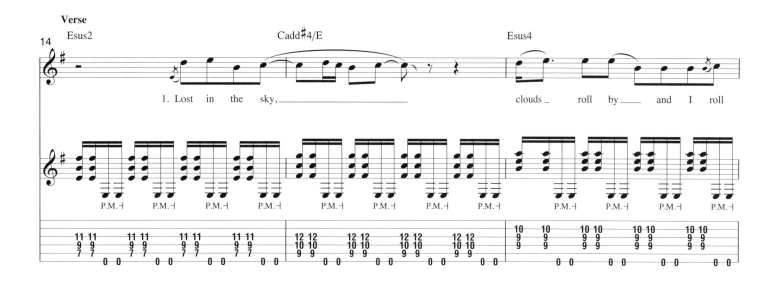

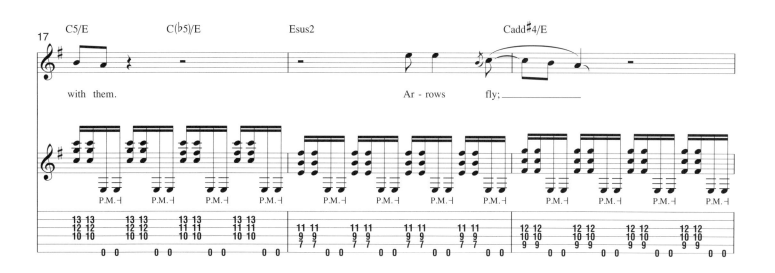

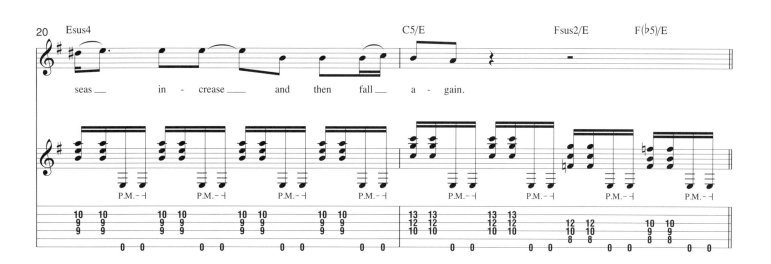

Figure 2—Pre-Chorus, Interlude

The next section beginning with the lyric, "This world is spinning around me," opens up into full-measure power chords, allowing the arrangement to breath freely while an arpeggiated clean guitar part can be heard lower in the mix, adding texture. Although this section is labeled as a *pre-chorus*, this term is a bit misleading here. The section has all the hallmarks of a *chorus*; it opens up big, the lyrics condense to a repeated motif, and it is followed by an interlude of building intensity, which then flows back into another verse. By contrast, a *pre-chorus* is a section that generally precedes a chorus and builds into it. So why is this section a pre-chorus rather than a chorus? There is a reason, but this won't become apparent until the next section.

The interlude picks up the pace in double time, as a 16th-note keyboard melody takes over. The keyboard part is notated for guitar if you would like to learn it; use strict alternate picking, noting the repeated syncopation effect created by the highest voice (B–C–E). A supportive guitar line (Gtr. 4) fills in below, but the most prominent guitar sound is the rhythm line, which drives underneath the 16th melodies with aggressive palm muting. Notice the harmonic liberties taken from the preceding progression, yet the interlude progression still functions within the same overall Em-with-added-C♯ tonality. Specifically, E and C♯ still undergird measures 9 and 11, respectively, but we find he has altered measures 10 and 12. Interestingly we also note that on the repetition, in measure 14, F♯5 replaces the D/A (F♯ is D's major 3rd, so not unrelated), and as we saw before, the section closes with F swapping in for C. In a nutshell, we have a great deal of continuity operating within these sections, even as a kaleidoscope of shifting detail provides nuance and variety.

Fig. 2

Full Band

Interlude
Double-time feel

Figure 3—Verse, Pre-Chorus, Interlude, Chorus

In true, highly progressive fashion, verse 2 bears no resemblance to the preceding verse. First, in an unexpected twist, it kicks off with a one-measure break of silence, riveting attention to the new vocal line. In measure 2, the rhythm guitar enters with a brand new motif played entirely on the low E string, picking up a similar syncopation effect as we saw happening in the interlude line of the keyboard. Play this with straight alternate picking.

Next, we have the "pre-chorus acting as chorus" once again, but instrumentally it is quite different this time around. The vocal is the same, and the keys hold down the four-bar progression, but drums take a snare-on-the-downbeat approach (effectively doubling the previous double-time and driving the energy up even higher) while the guitar works some low-register scale magic around the chord tones laid down in the keys. Maintain alternate picking such that a downstroke is played on each downbeat.

The interlude begins as a guitar solo but concludes quickly, acting as a peak moment and instrumental transition into the chorus. The lead opens in the key of A minor over the chords E5–F5. John begins on E's 5th (B), walks up to the ♭7th (D) diatonically, and then moves down to the F's major 3rd (A). And just as soon as you have adapted to this slow chord-tone melody, John hits a blazing 32nd-note ascent up to a high B. This is to be played with strict alternate picking. The scale is that of A natural minor until he hits the second string, with the notes D♯–E–F♯. This can be regarded as a chromatically altered three-note grouping, simply shifted down from the E–F–G that follows. That is, the notes that would be "inside" the key are E–F–G. So by first playing each of these three notes down a half step, and then rising (D♯–E–F♯ followed by E–F–G), we essentially have a chromatic approach tone rising to its target note. The only difference, however, is that here John is using all three pitches together as a "chromatic approach tone." This gives a little extra melodic tension to the line and keeps it from being a straight key run. A single chromatic approach tone (A♯) is used just before the last note in the solo, which is a more conventional application of this concept.

Under the sustaining final note of the solo, we have a 3/8 measure, courtesy of Mike Portnoy no doubt, having transformed repeated upbeats into a downbeat feel and moving forward on *that* as the new pulse. Very progressive. Yet it is worked in so flawlessly that one hardly notices this until you try to tap your foot to the pulse!

Then we finally come to the *real* chorus: the one with the title hook. And looking back, now we see why what initially appeared to be a chorus is labeled "pre-chorus." How many choruses can a song have, anyway? Perhaps two. Or we may label them "pre-chorus" and "chorus." In any case, what we are really seeing here are the limitations of the standard terms used in defining song structures. That is, we are seeing the fact that the progressive nature of Dream Theater is refusing to sit nicely within such conformities.

In any case, the chorus sits in large contrast to the rest of the song. First, the entire key center moves up to A (the IV chord of E) and holds in for three full measures. Yet, we can also see that, compositionally speaking, John has worked in some similarities to provide the needed continuity. One recurring harmonic quality we noted before was the presence of the major 6th (C♯ in the key of E), and here we see the same major 6th prominently in measure 25 (F♯ in the key of A). Another nod to the preceding progressions in E can be seen in measure 26, with a similar ♭VI–♭VII (F–G) move as heard in the pre-chorus. Never one to go for simple repetition when something more interesting can be done, on the second half of the chorus as the vocal melody repeats, John leaves the comfort of a big sustaining A5 power chord to climb up Am to F5, and B♭ (♭II) now acts as a pivot back to Em via a metal tritone twist.

Fig. 3

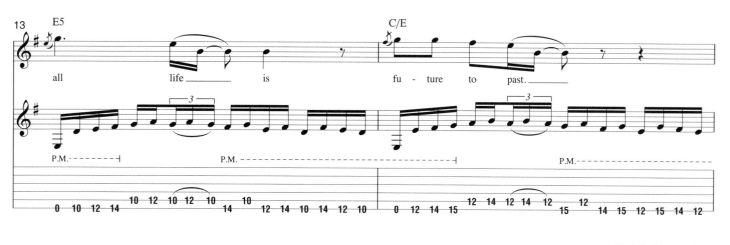

all   life _____ is   fu - ture to past. _____

End double-time feel

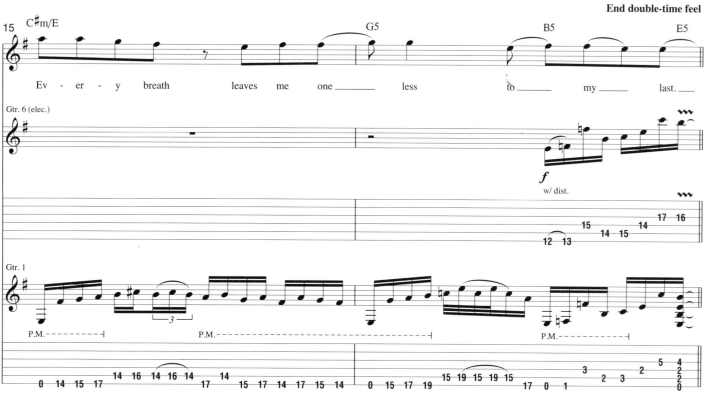

Ev - er - y breath   leaves me one _____ less   to _____ my   last. _____

Gtr. 6 (elec.)

Gtr. 1

Interlude

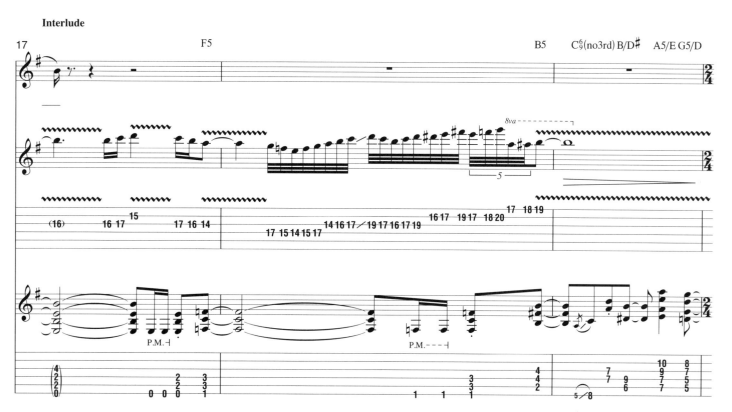

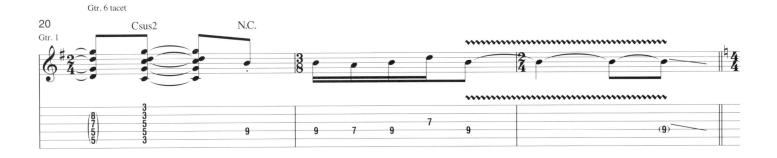

Chorus

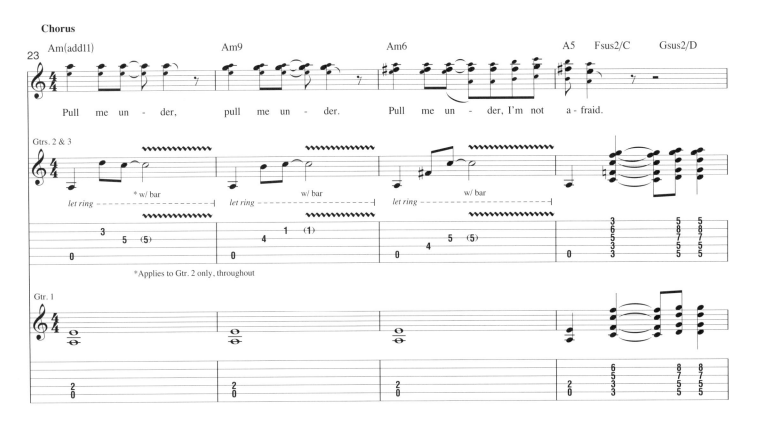

Pull me un - der, pull me un - der. Pull me un - der, I'm not a - fraid.

*Applies to Gtr. 2 only, throughout

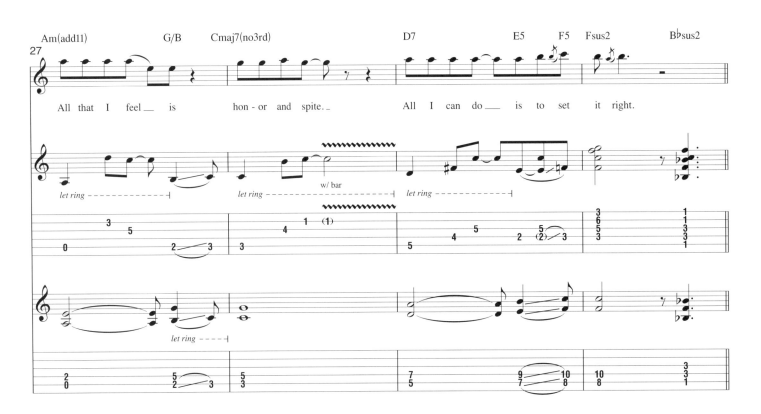

All that I feel __ is hon - or and spite. __ All I can do __ is to set it right.

Figure 4—Guitar Solo

At 6:06, the keyboard solo ends, and the lead guitar steps forward, playing over basically the same progression found in the first pre-chorus: E5–Csus2–C#sus2–G5–B5. John opens by quoting the melody heard in the vocal line previously with the lyric, "This world is spinning around me…" A descending scale run in measure 4 utilizes E Dorian, courtesy of incorporating C# into an Em context. These rhythmic figures of seven notes per beat are easiest to accomplish by simply "cramming in" the notes of the pattern as needed to target and land on the F# downbeat that begins beat 2, and again to land on the octave lower F# on beat 3. As beat 3 lands over a B5 power chord, where the F# is B's 5th, we hear this purposeful chord tone motion lend melodic power to the run.

The next phrase returns to the vocal melody, but this time he quotes it up an octave, raising the overall energy. In measure 7, over the C#sus2, John launches into a repeating lick in sextuplets. Straight alternate picking causes what is known as "outside picking" to occur as the transition between strings 1 and 2; that is, the pick approaches E on string 1 with an upstroke, then plays C# on string 2 with a downstroke, and then moves back to E on string 1 again with an upstroke (thereby approaching the string transition from "outside" the center point).

The next measure is a blazing 32nd-note legato run in E natural minor. We begin on F#, which is the underlying G5 chord's major 7th. Notice the recurring one-beat motif, which is sequenced to create the full run. The D note is sharped as we near the B5 chord, creating E harmonic minor. D# is B's major 3rd, which evokes a strong V–i cadence and gives us a nod toward the neo-classical sound.

Full Band

Slow Demo
Gtr. 6   meas. 7–9

Fig. 4

6:06

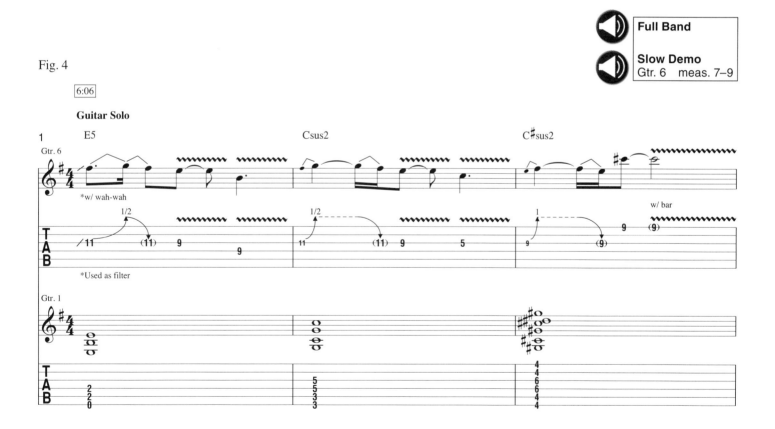

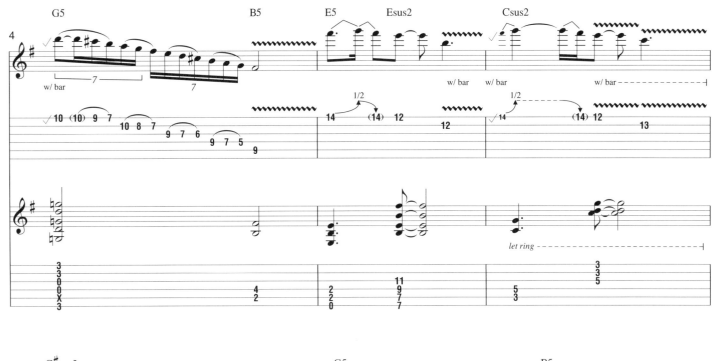

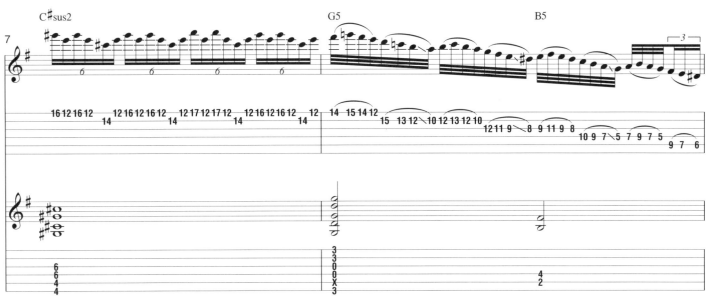

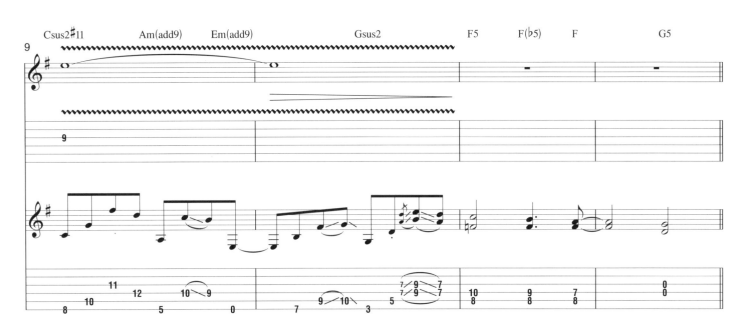

UNDER A GLASS MOON

(*Images and Words*, 1992)
Words and Music by Kevin LaBrie, Kevin Moore, John Myung,
John Petrucci and Michael Portnoy

Figure 5—Intro

"Under a Glass Moon" is track 6 on *Images and Words*. Lyrics are credited to John Petrucci. The song opens with a long intro in characteristic Dream Theater fashion, building up the instrumentation gradually. First we hear a lone guitar playing an octave melody (with very quiet keys added to thicken the texture slightly) and giving a kind of majestic "lone sentinel" feel. Arranged in four sections over a key center of F#, the tones of the melody are C#–F# (5–1), G#–E (2–b7), and B–D (4–b6), which at first imply an F# minor tonality, but then it shifts abruptly and ends on the bright major 3rd of F#, with B–A# (4–3). Taken together, the best scale to accommodate all these tones is 1–2–3–4–5–b6–b7, which is an exotic scale that goes by several different names, including the Hindustan (or Hindu) scale, Mixolydian b6 (which arises as the fifth mode of the melodic minor scale), or Aeolian dominant. The lower part of the scale is that of a standard major scale, while the upper part is that of natural minor.

In measure 9, John contrasts the preceding G# (2nd) with a quick G natural (b2nd), drawing out the darker, dramatic quality of the Spanish Flamenco (also known as Phrygian dominant) scale (1–b2–3–4–5–b6–b7).

Perhaps the most striking thing in this opening melody, however, is the progressive quality created by virtue of the first motif (measures 1–2) being rhythmically offset from the two phrases that follow. That is, the octave G#s in measure 2 act like pickup notes into the Es that follow, which land squarely on beat 1. Then at the end of measure 4, the octave B notes similarly act as a pickup to the following D5 on beat 1. However, if you go back to measures 1–2, you'll notice that there are no parallel pickup notes, rhythmically speaking. Yet as a melodic motif, the first C# octave notes here are clearly parallel to those later pickup notes. The effect this creates is a bit of rhythmic ambiguity. That is, one cannot be sure if beat "1" is really on C# (the first notes) or if C# is a pickup note, and the "1," rhythmically speaking, is actually on the F#s. If that were the case, we would have a 2/4 measure (dropping two beats out of the first motif) and throwing a nice progressive curve at the listener. Kicking off the song in this manner keeps the listener wondering what exactly is going on rhythmically and gives a kind of suspended, floating feel. All becomes a bit clearer at measure 11 when the drums enter. Yet still, this odd phrasing methodology adds a bit of rhythmic interest.

Next, the band builds further, adding a higher octave guitar part and increasing the majesty of the line before crunching down hard in measure 27 with a tight, driving rhythm as the chords evoke a strong F# Phrygian dominant tonality with the motif F#–G–F# (1–b2–1).

This is a good example of how John takes a fairly standard metal approach and throws in his characteristic progressive element to take it into new territory. First, notice how the second measure of the riff ends with a palm-muted "tag" of F#–G–F#–E (1–b2–1–b7). Then we see the riff repeated but with a slightly different ending of A–G–E–E–G–F#–E–E (b3–b2–b7–b7–b2–1–b7–b7). So far, this is a standard approach to metal riffing. The third riff repetition goes back to utilize the first ending tag, which again is not unusual. Next, however, John breaks with conformity and extends the 16th-note tag to keep right on rolling over what would normally be a fourth repetition of the riff. Added keys here also punch up the energy and make this almost an interlude "solo" moment, with all the instruments charging in unison.

The next evolution at measure 35 stretches out into experimental dissonances. The tonic note F# is now paired with its tritone C natural. The next chord G(b5) is likewise treated with its tritone D♭. This makes another iteration of the F#–G–F# motif, albeit over a longer time frame and "harmonized" with ♭5ths—very progressive harmonic ideas. The phrase completes with a higher voicing of F#(♭5) with applied sweep picking and ends with B(♭5).

Fig. 5

Full Band

Slow Demo
Gtrs. 1 & 2   meas. 31–38

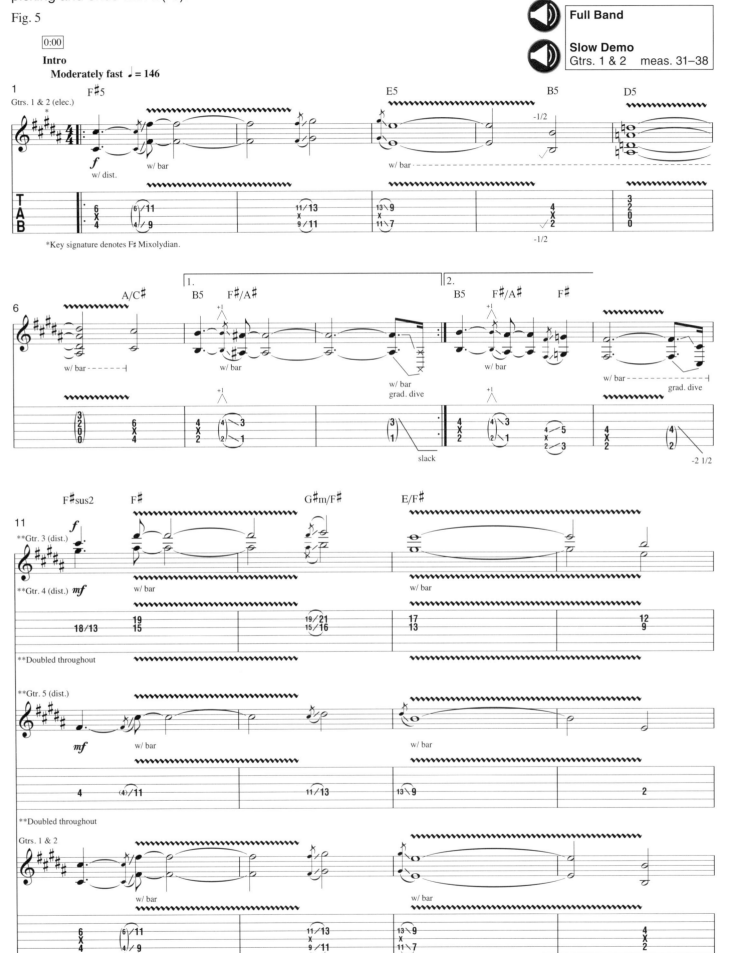

*Key signature denotes F# Mixolydian.

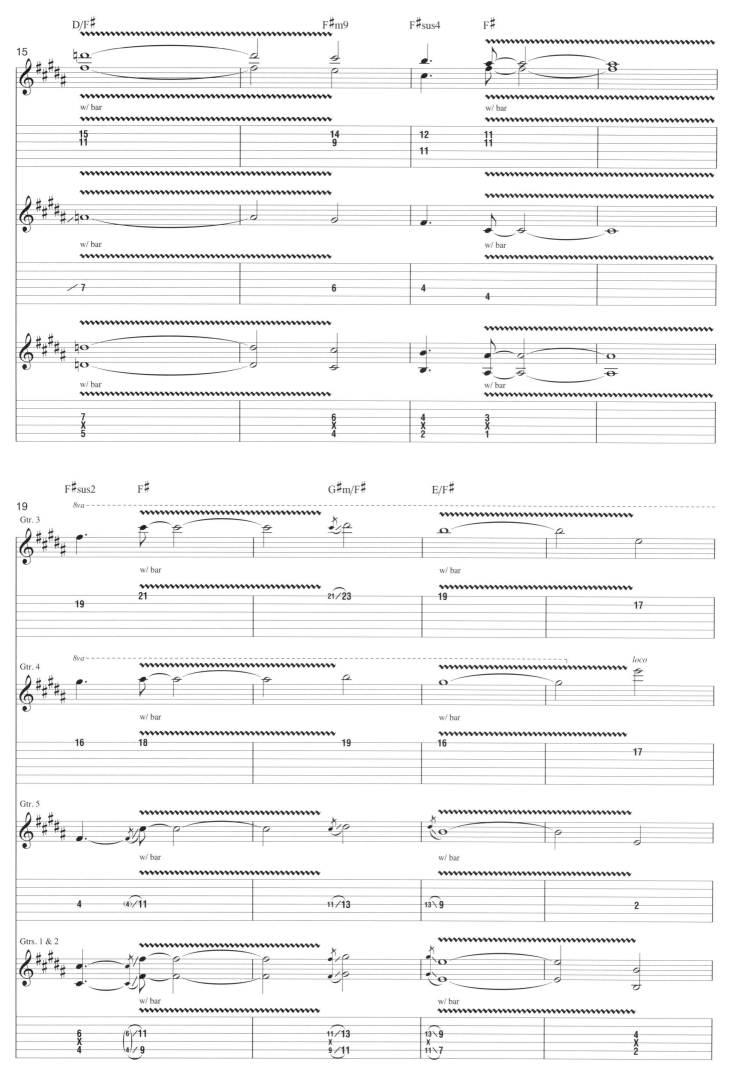

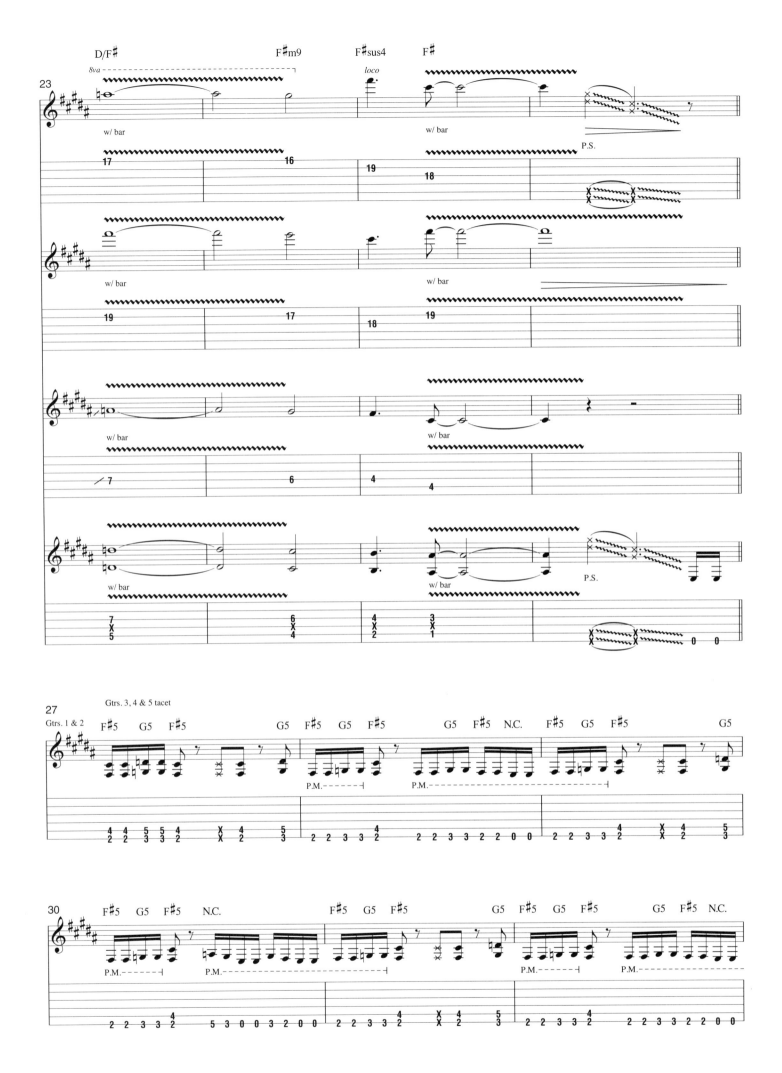

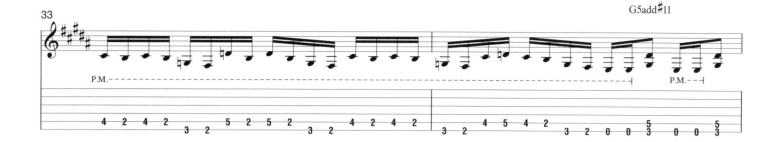

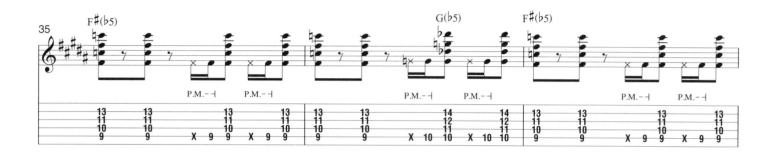

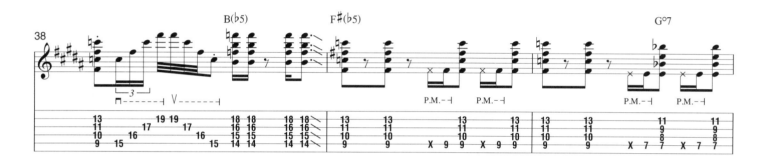

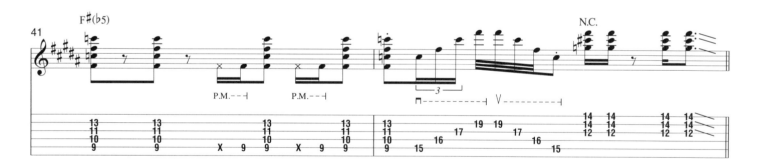

Figure 6—Chorus

The chorus section highlights John's intricate rhythm work, with palm-muted pedal tones and chord jabs that move incredibly fast. Slow down the section and piece it together, only working up the speed as you find it comfortable to do so. Be sure to apply a solid palm mute to the indicated notes, but lift your palm fully on the chords to allow them to jump out with accents in good metal fashion.

The chorus changes key to C# minor and opens on C#5 (implied C#m), which is the i chord. So harmonically, we have C#5–Asus2–F#sus2, which is a i–♭VI–iv progression with the coloration of added/suspended 9th (2nd) tones over the A5 and F#5. Completing measure 4, we see a single-note line sporting chromatically ascending tones followed by a sharp, syncopated chord jab on the decidedly jazzy D7#9 chord.

In the second four-measure phrase, we see a similar progression, although the chord-change points have been moved with regard to timing. The significant chords are C#5 again, followed by A (split measure moving to its relative minor F#m) and then Bsus2, which corresponds loosely to i–♭VI–♭VII. The phrase closes with a moment on G5–F5, skirting first a half step above and then a half step below what would be the v chord, creating an odd melodic tension in the rhythm line.

Fig. 6

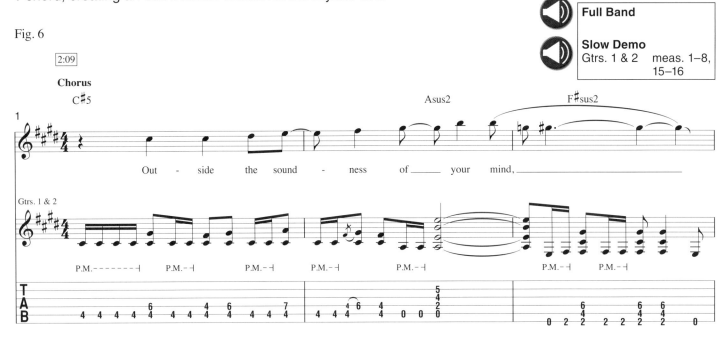

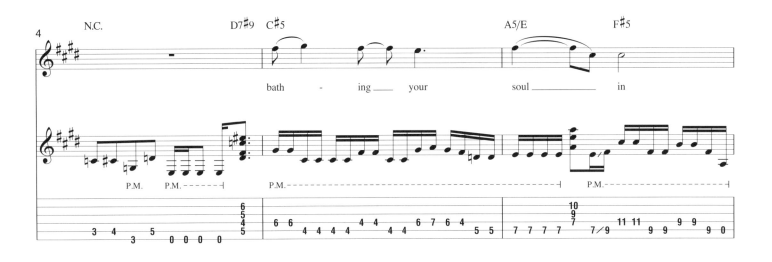

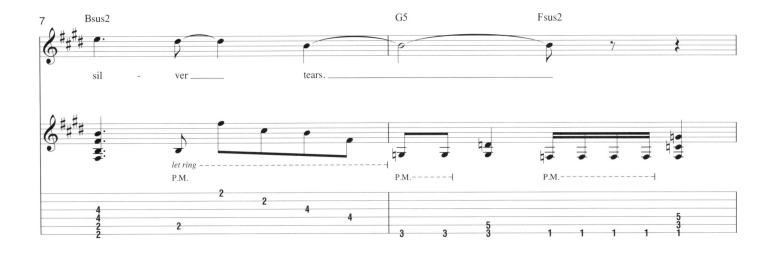

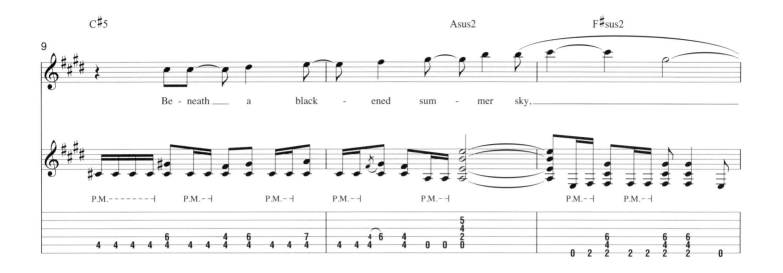

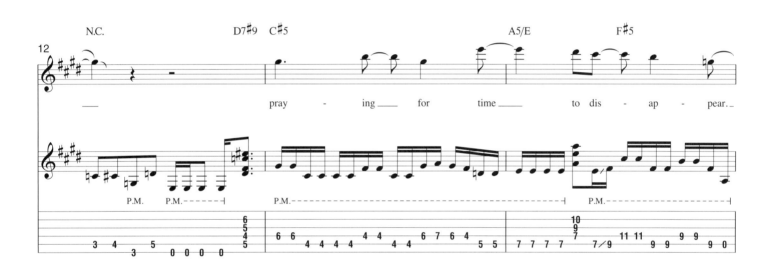

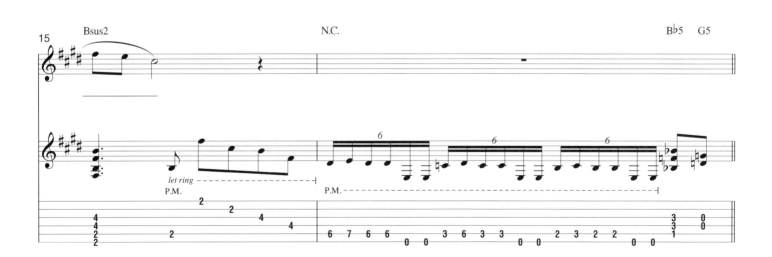

Figure 7—Guitar Solo

In May, 2014, "Under a Glass Moon" was awarded the 98th position in the *100 Greatest Guitar Solos* poll by *Guitar World* magazine. It is certainly one of John's shining solo moments, full of trademark passages. Let's take a closer look.

The solo section takes place over long sustaining chords, four measures on each, following the progression F#m–E–C#m–B. But with each chord sustaining so long, John is free to focus on the chord tones of each to a greater degree than rock soloists typically utilize.

First, he opens with an oblique bend chord dyad. Over the keynote F#, we have B at the twelfth fret bent up a full step to C# and played together with E on the first string. C# and E add up to 5th and b7th over the F# root, filling out the underlying F#m tonic chord to an F#m7. Semi-harmonics created by digging the thumb in close to the string while picking, combined with a quick bend-release and large position shifts on a single string, give this line a unique, sparkling quality. At measure 3, he pauses on D# (major 6th), lending a bit of a lift and adding a moment of brightness to the tonality at this point. In fact, all of measure 3 can be seen as a "decorative major 6th," harmonically speaking, as it both begins and ends on this pitch, emphasizing it strongly. Sandwiched in between the pitches we see (arranged in ascending series) C#–D#–F#–G#–B–C#–D#–E, which corresponds to 5–6–1–2–4–5–6–b7 relative to F#, spelling out the Mixolydian mode (except for the missing major 3rd), delivered in a largely pentatonic shape. Measure 4 completes the phrase with an abrupt jump up into 12th position for a quick Emaj7 arpeggio descent. Note that, although E does show up as the following underlying chord (John is anticipating this move), over F# this Emaj7 actually becomes extended jazz harmony (F#13). That is, the notes of Emaj7, which are E–G#–B–D# (1–3–5–7), when placed over an F# root become F#–E–G#–B–D# (1–b7–9–11–13).

The second four-measure phrase over E (beginning at measure 5) opens with John nailing the open low E string, making the underlying chord change even more prominent. Head's up! Chord change! The contrast of jazz harmony in the preceding 13 chord to utter simplicity here is also quite refreshing, and this low E rolls out naturally and seamlessly from the descending Emaj7 arpeggio that preceded it, connecting this new four-measure phrase on E. Next, building on this simplicity, John ascends in natural harmonics with an E major triad: first E (root), then G# (3rd), and B (5th). An added vibrato bar wobble connects into the next measure's "backwards climb." The next measure places the spotlight on A# (#4), drawing out the distinct quality of E Lydian. (Staying within the modal family of F# Mixolydian, the b7 tone E becomes the root of the E Lydian mode.) The last measure over E is a blazing diatonic run coming straight down the E major scale.

Things get funky over the next four bars on C#m, and a nice blues run concludes this section. Four bars over B are next, and for added variety, the band behind John changes it up with a series of highly offbeat accents. John opts for B Lydian, beginning with a fairly straight line rhythmically to hold it all together. Then he pushes the rhythm further with a high B, descending two-octave sweep, and a jump back to the middle B octave. An ascending line in B major connects directly into the next phrase, which is back to the opening chord, F#m.

A very "Vai-esque" repeat-slide lick comes next, with sliding 5th shapes in a hemiola-style (three against two) rhythm that give and interesting rhythmic effect. This gives way to an F# minor pentatonic box 1 lick in standard glam rock style in the next measure—something we might expect from the likes of George Lynch of Dokken or Warren DeMartini of Ratt. Next, he flows directly into a descending box 1 lick with added chromaticism and ends on the major 3rd (A#) in a nod toward Randy Rhoads. Yet all these elements are fused seamlessly, creating a nice contrast of tones and stylistic effect.

A second foray over E is next, and we see John go off on another tangent via a rhythmically inspired motif with tapping and bends, á la Steve Vai. Then we see a brilliant use of perfectly executed sweep picking and tapping.

Four measures over C#m are next with some crazy whammy bar antics, including a flutter created by lightly depressing the bar and then slipping your finger off the end of it, allowing it to shake as it returns to pitch. (This only works on Floyd Rose-style floating trem systems.)

The ultimate alternate picking confrontation happens over the last two measures of B, with the unusual rhythmic figures of 11 notes per half note. This is more the result of cramming in notes and landing "on your feet" at the end by virtue of feeling the underlying rhythm. Notice, in fact, that the lick is chromatic sets of four, arranged in groups of three each. First, we see strings 3–2–1, then 1–2–3, then 3–4–5. The last group only allows time for two patterns, both on string 6 with a position shift. Therefore, it may be more appropriate to feel this lick (and practice with a metronome) as if it were eighth-note triplets, with each note of the triplet being actually composed of four notes. So if you took only the first 12 notes, you would feel the triplet occurring on the three notes played by your first finger. Of course, this rhythm is slightly falling behind the pulse in the actual song performance, but it would be the best way to approach getting a handle on this lick from a practice standpoint.

Full Band

Slow Demo
Gtr. 6   meas. 1–33

Fig. 7

Guitar Solo

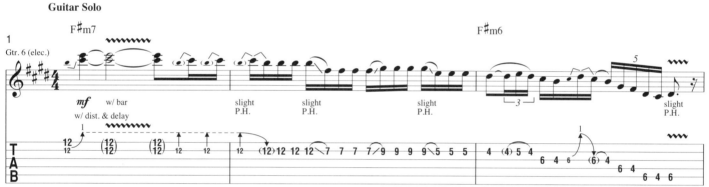

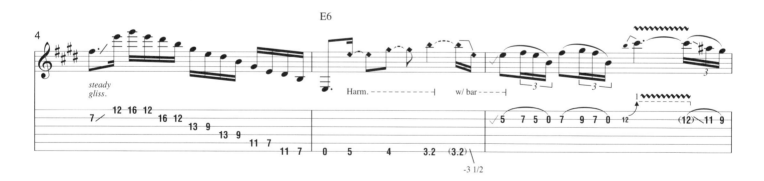

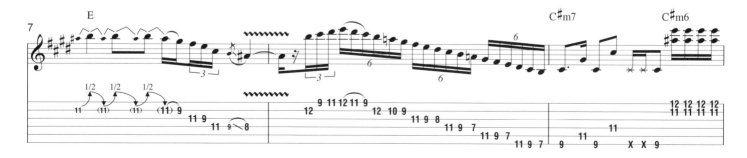

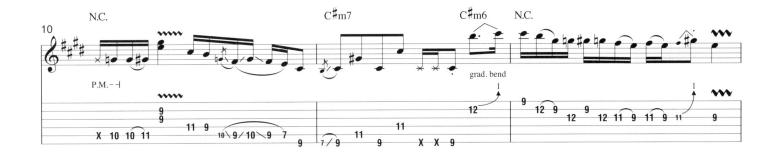

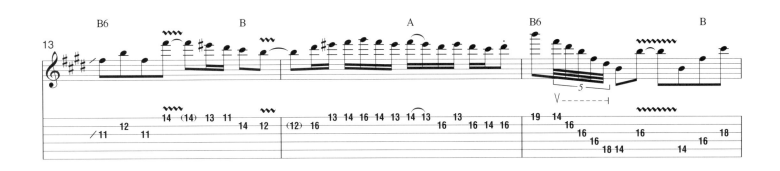

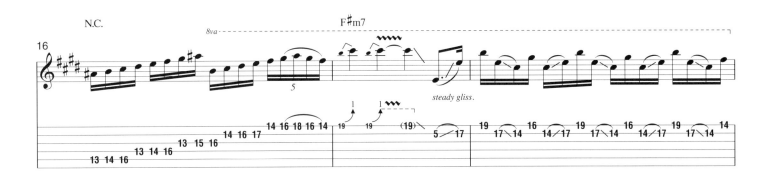

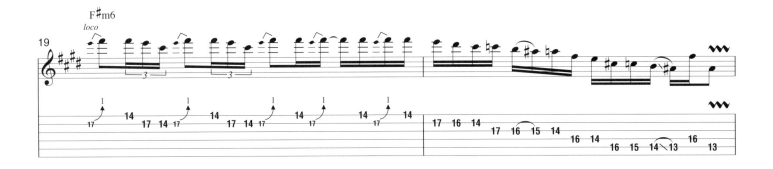

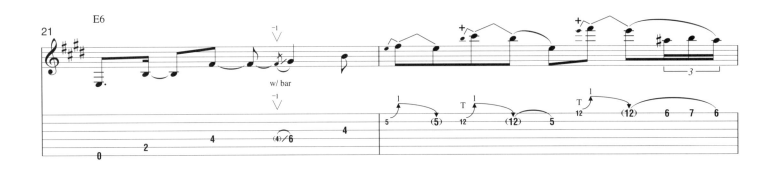

UNDER A GLASS MOON

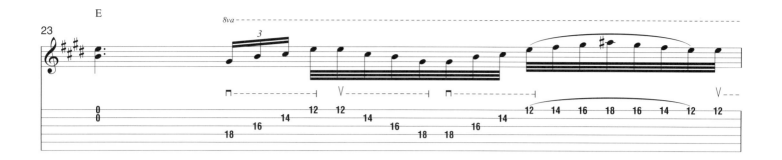

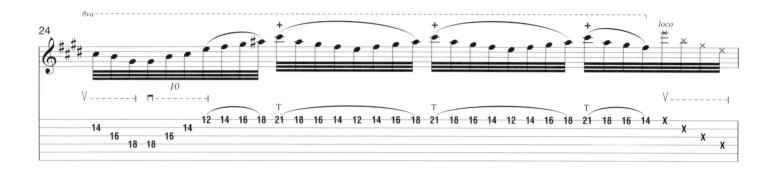

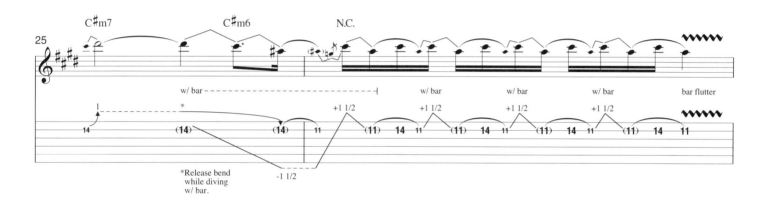

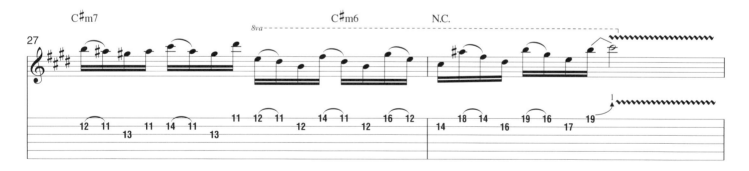

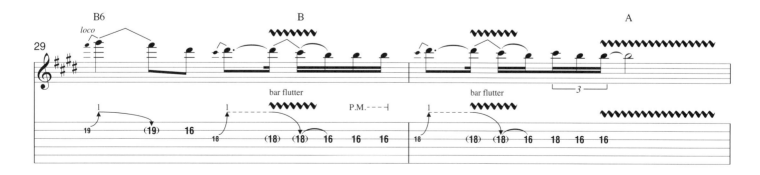

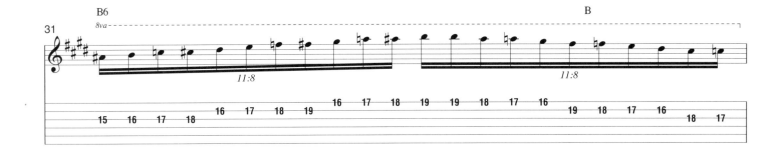

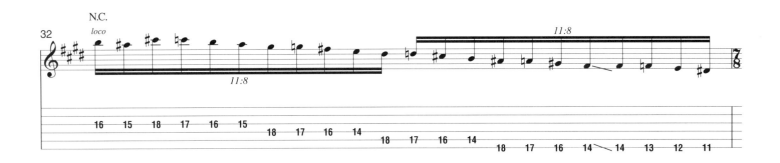

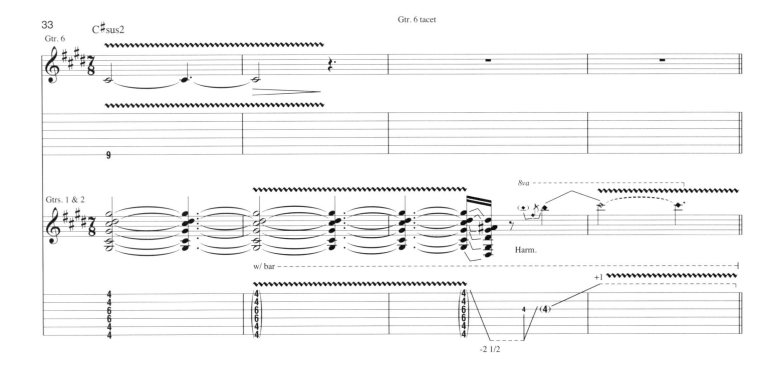

EROTOMANIA

(*Awake*, 1994)

Music by Kevin LaBrie, Kevin Moore, John Myung, John Petrucci and Michael Portnoy

After the success of *Images and Words*, the label was putting some pressure on the band to recreate the success of "Pull Me Under" with another single. Also, due to the advent of grunge and metal, the label was pushing for a heavier, darker sound. Petrucci went to the seven-string for the first time and focused on a more riff-based writing approach, which would further cement the band as *the* iconic fusion of metal and progressive. He is quoted in Rich Wilson's 2009 biography of the band, *Lifting Shadows: The Authorized Biography of Dream Theater*, as saying "I think [*Awake*] paved the way for many of our strongest and heaviest later songs like 'A Change of Seasons,' 'The Glass Prison,' and 'The Dark Eternal Night.'" Vocalist James LaBrie also went for a much more aggressive tone than on *Images and Words*.

In the sessions themselves, Mike Portnoy recalled, "It never came to blows, but there was a lot of bickering over every single element, like the fine details of what the third note on the 64th bar should be." Added to the pressure was the time crunch. Portnoy explains, "Somebody once said that you have your whole life to prepare for your first album and have about two months to prepare the follow-up, and that was very much the situation we faced in early 1994." Nevertheless, although the album did not materialize a single of the same commercial success as "Pull Me Under," they clearly rose to the challenge artistically and revealed a new, more aggressive Dream Theater. The album peaked at number 32 on the *Billboard* Top 200 chart.

"Erotomania" is a six-plus minute instrumental piece that serves as Part 1 of a larger suite entitled "A Mind Beside Itself," with a host of dissonances, chromaticism, parallel modal tonalities, and odd time signatures.

Figure 8—A, B, C

After the keyboard/organ moves through the four-measure intro phrase one time, the guitar kicks in with a climbing single-note motif in 5/4 time. The key is open to interpretation against the keyboard's dissonant tone clusters. The chords in measure 5 could be seen as outlining F♯ Phrygian (with added chromatic G♯ on the sixth string ascent) and then closing a half step up from F♯ on the G accent point. (The guitar plays only the G root, while the C and D appears in the keyboard part, the chord symbols indicating the composite chord Gsus4.) The guitar shifts up two frets to repeat the same sequence in G♯ Phrygian, closing on A at the end of measure 6. Alternatively, the opening F♯ line could also be interpreted as outlining a D major chord in first inversion, and the next measure would then be seen as an E major chord—an interpretation strengthened by the E to G♯ pickup at the start of measure 6. In this case, we would see it as the progression D/F♯–G–E/G♯–A. Either way, the important thing is to see the overall chromatic ascent operating within it (F♯–G–G♯–A).

Measures 7 and 8 return to repeat these measures, but with a time signature modification. A single eighth note is dropped out of at the end of the measure, transforming 5/4 (ten eighth notes) into 9/8 (nine eighth notes). To accomplish this, the pulse must hit two consecutive eighths: the last eighth note in the 9/8 measure and the first eighth of the next 5/4 measure. The eighth-note count through measures 3, 4, and 5 would be "**1** & **2** & **3** & **4** & **5** & **1** & **2** & **3** & **4** & **5 1** & **2** & **3** & **4** & **5** &." To play this with a metronome, set it to click at the tempo of the eighth notes—not the standard quarter-note pulse—and tap your foot with every other click except where the two taps happen back to back. At that point (5 1), tap out two successive clicks, both as downbeats, and then continue as before. Until you get the feel of this odd rhythmic technique, dial the tempo way back and "map it out," slowly attaching each downbeat and upbeat to a note and tapping the numbered pulse carefully. Speed will come quickly with practice, and eventually counting measures like this will become second nature for you.

A new riff enters at measure 13, spelling out the E Lydian mode. Measure 14 moves chromatically, weaving around D and falling toward G. Beats 3 and 4 move quickly through G and F, which leans heavily on the tonic, E, temporarily implying E Phrygian. Measure 15 switches back to E Lydian. This quick swapping between parallel modal tonalities is another hallmark of the band's pioneering progressive metal technique. Finally, to complete the phrase, the missing eighth-note measure (9/8) is forgone; in its place, we see two measures of straight 4/4 time (eight beats). After so much rhythmic oddity, a few bars of straight time feels refreshingly unusual and becomes a contrasting effect for the extended tag that marks the end of this riff. The end of the riff includes a high guitar harmony playing 6ths.

At the C section, we get some even crazier time signature mischief. As if to direct the listener's focus squarely on the unpredictability of the timing element, the notes are simplified to make a repeating, descending chromatic sequence. (The operating principle is that by removing change in one element, the composer directs attention more clearly on to the changing element, which in this case is rhythmic chaos.) Count the dotted quarter as three eighths on a single beat, as if it were written in 12/8 time. So you have three "trip-l-et" counts, and the last one is only a double. The next measure gives just two trip-l-et counts and two doubles. The count would be this, with the notes changing on the rhythmic emphasis of the bold notes: **1** 2 3, **1** 2 3, **1** 2 3, **1** 2, **1** 2 3, **1** 2 3, **1** 2, **1** 2.

At measures 27–28, the band builds on this unsettled rhythmic base, by syncopating it and setting keys and guitars in rhythmic opposition. Again, the easiest way to approach this is to feel it with the same trip-l-et, trip-l-et, trip-l-et, doub-le, trip-l-et, trip-l-et, doub-le, doub-le as before. This time, however, you will be playing some of the subdivisions of the beat, unlike before, where you played only on the compound beats. Finally, at measures 29–30, the band takes the same timing mayhem up to a higher energy level with full power chords grinding out the 3–3–3–2 and 3–3–2–2 rhythms.

Fig. 8

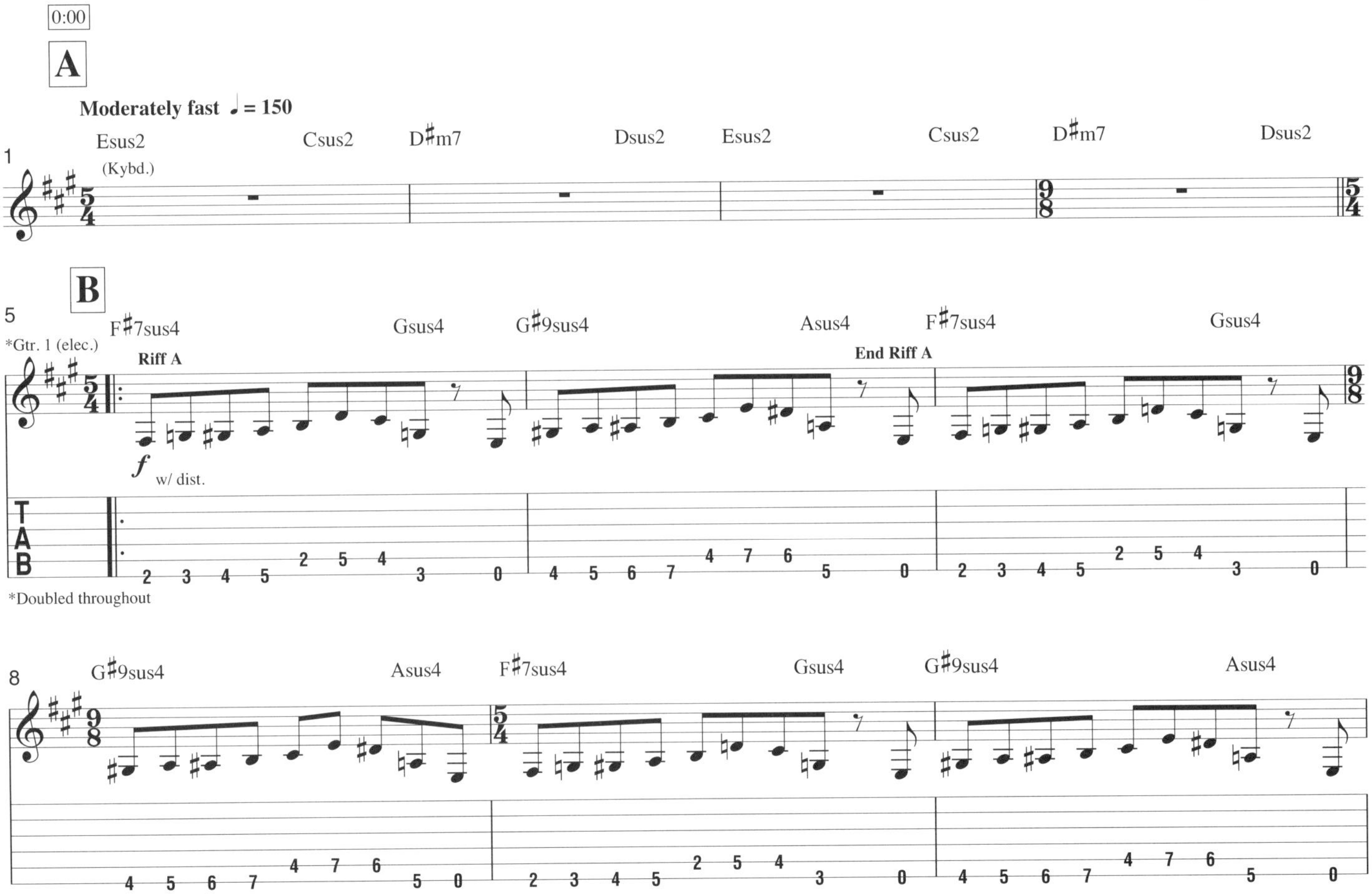

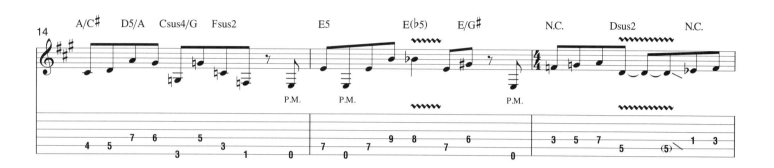

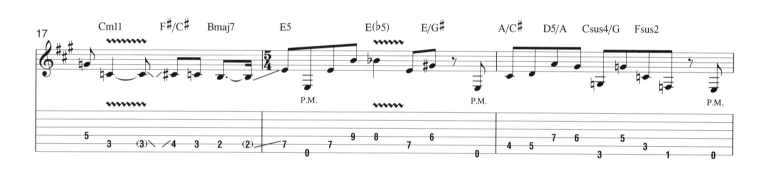

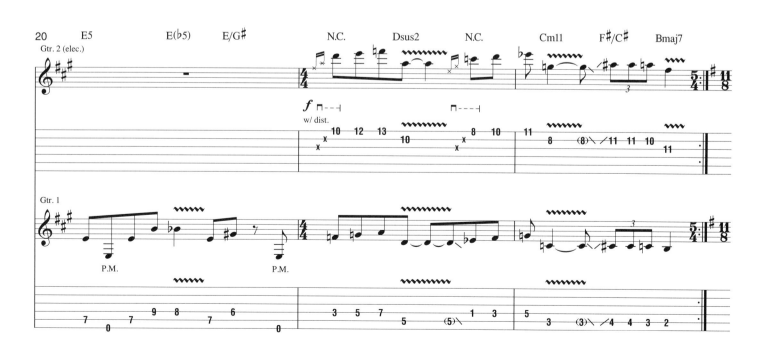

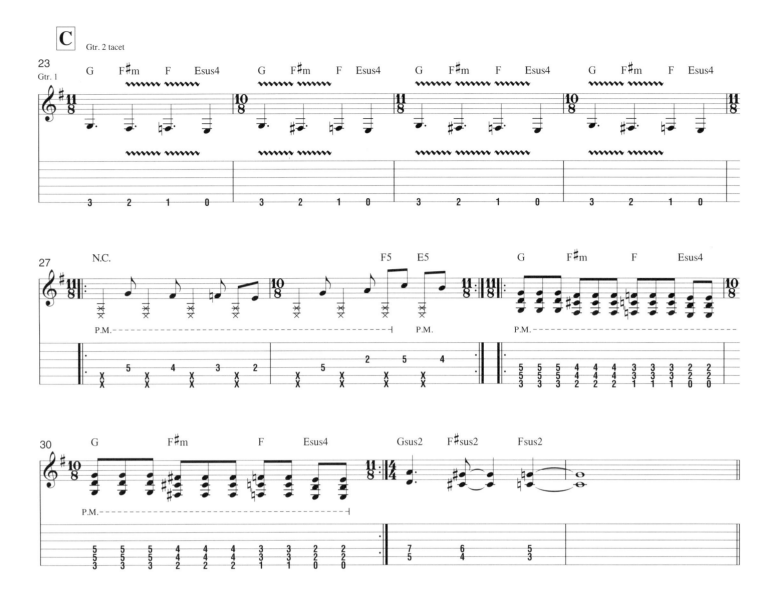

Figure 9—D (Guitar Solo 1)

Soloing over 5/4 time is a trick in and of itself, let alone making sense of such a chromatically tattered harmony. John begins slowly and simply and builds. An F# unison bend over an F# Phrygian line, followed by a unison D bend over G, acts to reinforce the rhythmic aspect of the underlying riff. This is a good, safe starting point to ease the listener in before we get off the beaten track, which happens soon enough.

In measure 2, John continues with the unison bend motif before outside tones wind around and target the prominent A note, which corresponds to the ending chord of this measure. A quick A major run on beat 5 acts as a pickup into the next measure for the riff's next repeat.

John hits E (♭7th) at the start of measure 3, over F#m again, creating an F#m7 composite tonality. Angular 4th intervals come next, with doubled "down-up" picking on each note establishing a strikingly unusual motif. This is followed by a stinging G note, again, directly over the G accent point in the underlying riff. Here, we can see that a good amount of the weirdness of this solo is in fact due to the oddity of the underlying riff itself, which John is following quite specifically and just developing a bit. At measure 4, he maintains his angular 4th interval "double picked" motif and then begins to repeat it down an octave, interrupting this to play an Asus2 arpeggio over the rhythm's accented A chord at the close of the measure.

Measure 5 slows to seven notes, so we can really take in the melodic twists and turns. Unexpected G octaves flow into F#–D#–A#–D# in measure 6. A shape that would usually indicate D# minor (♭3–1–5–1), over G#m it actually becomes (♭7–5–9–5), forming a G#m9 chord harmonically. The extended tones, with large melodic leaps, act to make this strange world even stranger.

Measure 7 uses the F#m box 1 area in 14th position for a diatonic F# Phrygian run with added chromaticism. In fact, there is so much chromatic motion that it may be hard to see the diatonic mode here, but remove the chromatic passing tones (A♭ and E♭) in beats 1 and 2, and you will see it. The last beat of the measure goes fully chromatic. Measure 8 starts with a stinging F# interrupting the rhythmic chromaticism only long enough to again emphasize the ♭7th (as in measure 3) before another fast ambiguous lick whose final note, B, is a noticeably unresolved 9th over the underlying A chord.

Full Band

Slow Demo
Gtr. 2   meas. 1–8

Fig. 9

1:49

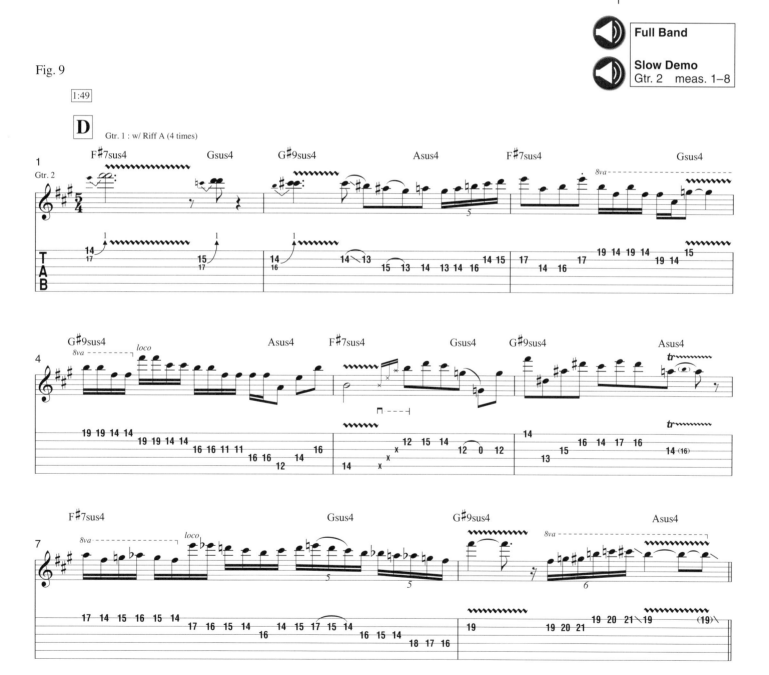

Figure 10—F (Clean section)

With a nod toward a classical influence, the texture changes abruptly for a low dynamic moment in the piece. The progression G#m–F#–B–C#m (i–♭VII–♭III–iv) is followed by E–F#–E–F# (♭VI–♭VII–♭VI–♭VII), and then all of this is repeated. The second time around, the guitar adds open E and B sustaining tones as it moves up through different inversions of the chord tones of the progression.

Fig. 10

Full Band

2:38

F

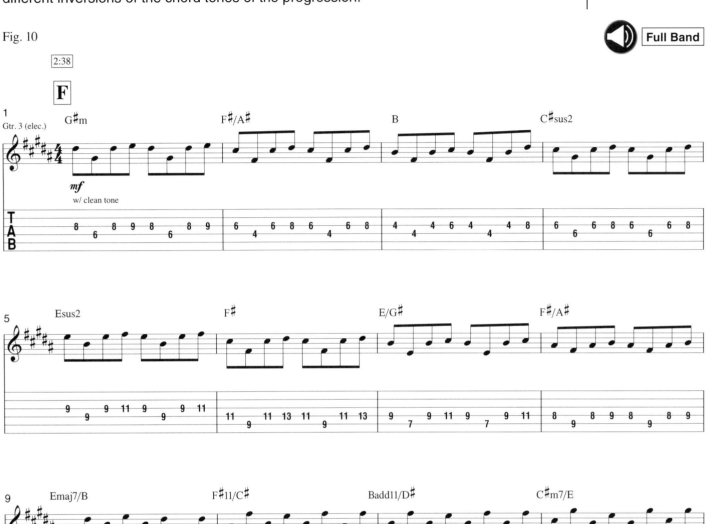

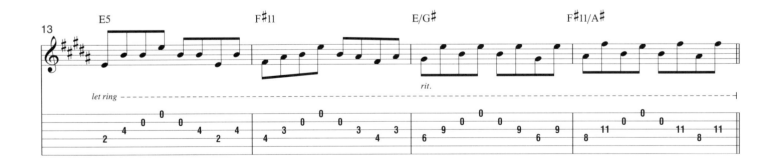

Figure 11—J, K, L (Guitar Solo 3)

Section J begins with a reprise of the section C time signature motif. John first plays pinch harmonics on the descending, single-note, chromatic passage underneath a keyboard melody. In measure 3, he adds a palm-muted version of the part shifted up an octave for a measure and a beat before breaking into an arpeggiated variation. This flows seamlessly into a baroque-inspired moment at measures 5 and 6 (apart from the progressive time signature aspect).

Measure 8 goes into straight 3/4 time with a series of full stops and quick, short descending runs, sending us deeper into the baroque-classical period. A long ascending, sequenced run in sextuplets acts as a cadenza and transitions into section K. Use strict alternate picking throughout.

Section K gives us a Dream Theater rendition (if not quotation) of early 18th century baroque composer Antonio Vivaldi, with a series of descending arpeggio lines built upon a motif of grace notes, pull-offs, and doubled notes arranged in a somewhat syncopated fashion. The progression makes prominent use of diminished 7th and dominant 7th chords to create strong "classical style" resolutions. We begin with Dm, which is twisted to become a fully diminished 7th chord as we descend. At first, it would appear that we have a D°7 (and we do), but fully diminished chords can be named with any of the four notes as the root (D°7, B°7, A♭°7 or G#°7, F°7—all use the same pitches). In classical music, standard practice is to name the diminished chord by looking backwards from its target chord. Since the chord that follows is actually C major, the "D°7" is properly labeled as a B°7; it pulls up a half step to resolve to its target, C.

C major gives way to D7 (low to high: A–C–D–F#–A–C), which is very nearly another diminished chord and acts essentially in the same manner. (If you raise the root of any dominant 7th chord a half step, you have a fully diminished 7th.) D7 generally wants to resolve to G, but in this case, we wind up resolving to B, G's major 3rd. This flows nicely, though, as we may expect to hear G major in first inversion (G/B) at that point. The B, however, is immediately converted into a slippery °7 itself, resolving to Am in measure 13. With A as its target, the correct label of this B°7 is actually G#°7. Then Am shifts abruptly into A7, setting up the final dominant cadence (V–i) to pull us back to Dm where we began. The whole sequence, then, is a tight circular pattern revolving around Dm.

At measures 14–15, John contrasts this with a broad, sweeping melodic line acting as a nice breathing space. The trills, however, still maintain the classical decorative feel as the progression utilizes fifth motion from Dm to G, followed by Em to A. This is interrupted at measure 17 with an intense, descending one-beat motif on a final extended Em chord, utilizing E Phrygian. The pattern is seven notes per beat via half a beat of 32nd notes followed by a 16th-note triplet. To enable this to be picked consistently, start with a downstroke on the first 32nd note. After the hammer and pull, the next note should be picked with another downstroke—not an upstroke as you might expect for 32nd notes. This allows the last triplet to be picked up, down, up, so we are ready to hit the next beat beginning with another downstroke. Measures 18–21 extend the cadenza upward.

Section L is a sort of quintuplet exercise, playing in five notes per beat. John approaches the line with a very pattern-based, mechanistic view. Notice that the lowest and highest notes of each quintuplet fall on the downbeat in every case. By maintaining this approach, he makes it a bit easier to get the five-note-per-beat rhythm. Simply feel the lowest and highest notes as if they were "accent points" (on each downbeat) and cram in the intervening notes as needed to get there on time. Using strict alternate picking in "fives" like this; the lowest note of each pattern will be played with a downstroke, and the highest note falls on an upstroke each time. Later, the pattern changes somewhat, but still the "fives" are easily felt due to the contour of the line reinforcing every fifth note as an accent, or "turning" point.

Fig. 11

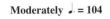

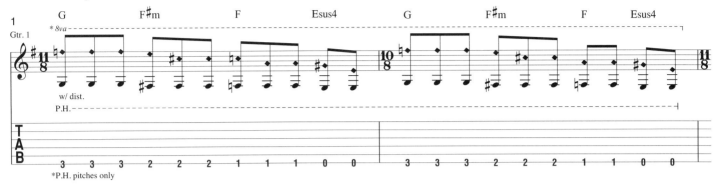

*P.H. pitches only

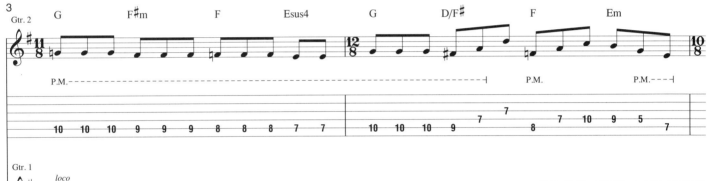

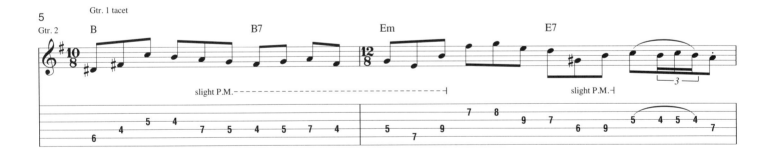

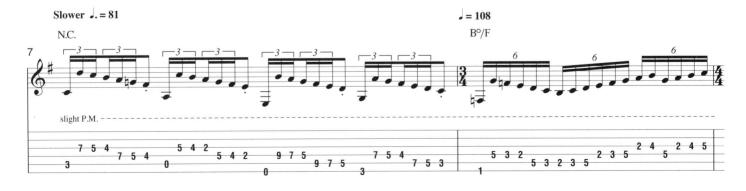

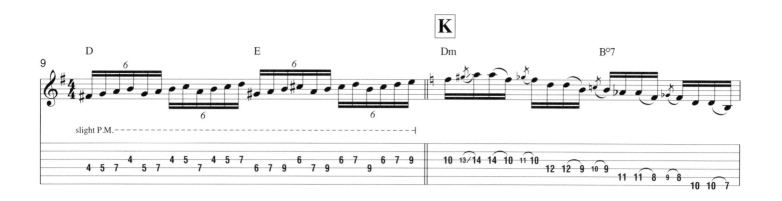

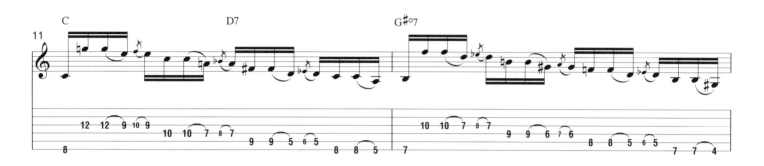

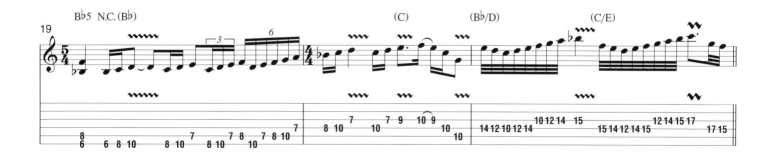

Moderately fast ♩ = 150

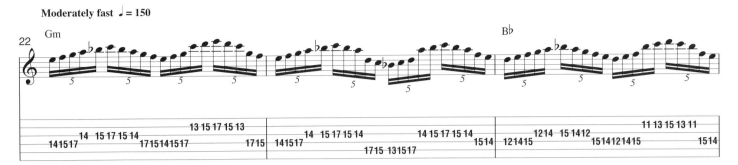

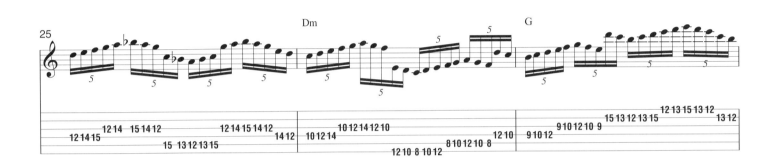

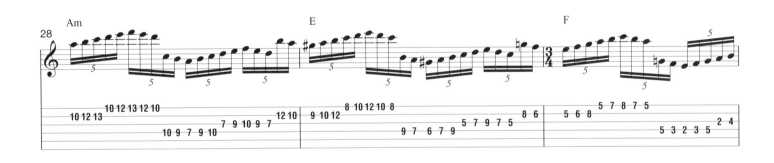

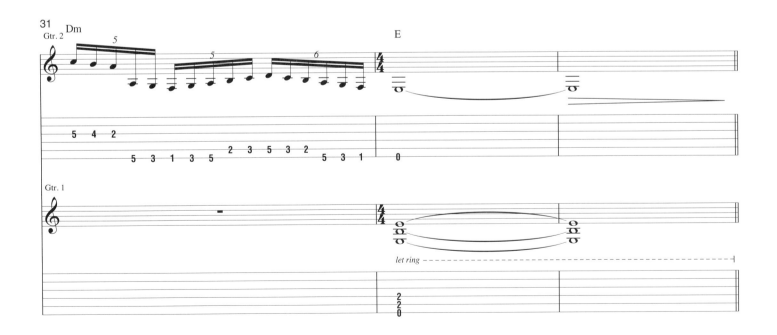

FATAL TRAGEDY

(*Metropolis, Pt. 2: Scenes from a Memory*, 1999)
Words and Music by John Petrucci, Michael Portnoy, John Myung, Jordan Rudess and Kevin LaBrie

Dream Theater's fifth studio album, *Metropolis, Pt. 2: Scenes from a Memory*, came out in 1999. It was actually a sequel to the song "Metropolis, Pt. 1: The Miracle and the Sleeper" from the 1992 album, *Images and Words*. Originally no sequel was ever intended, but fans had begun asking for this. A 21-minute instrumental demo of "Metropolis, Pt. 2" had in fact been recorded for *Falling to Infinity* (1997), but it did not make the album. This demo was later released, however, and many of the motifs that did make the final album in 1999 can be heard on it.

Keyboardist Jordan Rudess also joined the band for this album, replacing Derek Sherinian. Rudess had played with Petrucci and Portnoy in the metal/jazz fusion super-group Liquid Tension Experiment, formed by Mike Portnoy in 1997. As they had found writing with Rudess very easy, they brought the idea to the rest of the band to have him come on board with Dream Theater full time. The others agreed, and Sherinian was let go via a conference call, described by Petrucci and Portnoy as an "uncomfortable and unattractive situation."

Figure 12—Interlude

"Fatal Tragedy" is Act 1, Scene 3, Part II on the album, appearing as CD track 6. The interlude at 2:06 picks up the momentum in characteristic Dream Theater style. Outlining a B–Em (V–i) progression, we see a single-note motif in 7/8 time. The odd rhythm felt here is caused by the "missing" final eighth note of the measure, which can make the two tense organ chords in the 2/4 measure that follows feel somewhat like upbeats. Instead, however, "double tap" beat 4 (the last eighth note) of the 7/8 measure and beat 1 of the 2/4 measure at the speed of consecutive eighth notes. The single-note motif then shifts to wind around the next chord, Em.

Fig. 12

Interlude

Moderately fast ♩ = 140

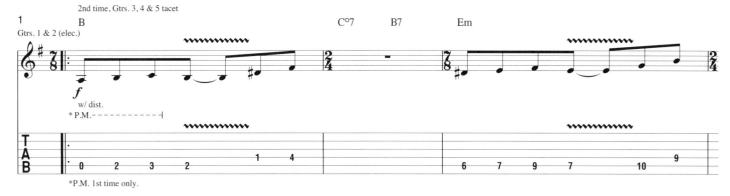

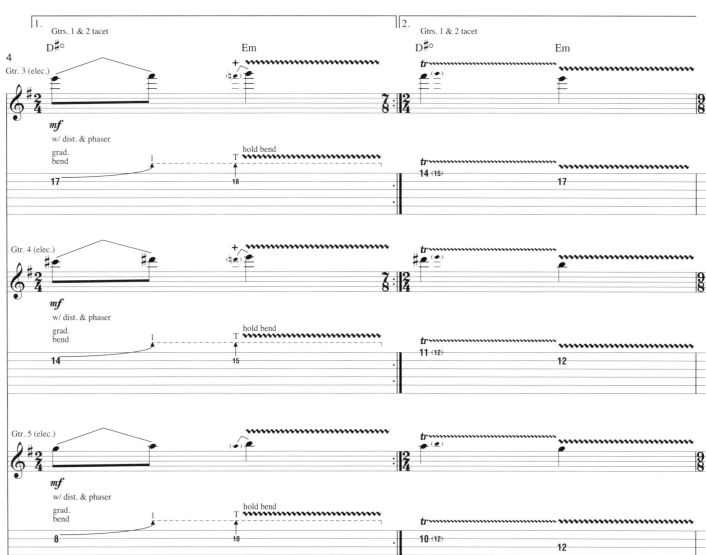

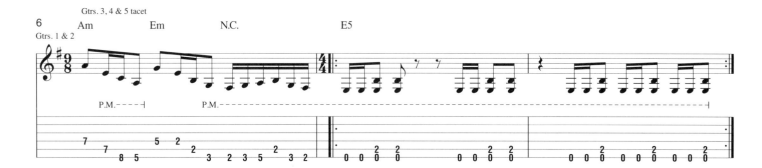

44

FATAL TRAGEDY

Figure 13—Verse

At 2:51, the verse evolves into a moderately paced walking eighth-note line, with occasional "double picked" 16th gallops. Of particular significance, notice the rising melodic contour found in the highest notes of the two-measure pattern. These higher notes, initially found at the fourth beat of measure 1, act as syncopated accents. Measures 3–4 essentially repeat measures 1–2, except the melodic contour found in these accent notes rises higher. Measures 5–6 take it even higher, now against a sustained Em pad in the keys. Measure 7 emphasizes Em with a power walk up the E minor blues scale, which then turns to harmonic minor at D#–F#–E (7–2–1), playing off the B–Em (V–i) cadence. Measure 8 counterbalances with a descending Em line. In particular, look at the two-note motif occurring at the start of beats 2, 3, and 4. First we have D–E (♭7–1), then B–E (5–1), and then G–E (♭3–1), spelling out an Em7 with chromatics sprinkled in between. The final two notes are accomplished simply by shifting the four-fret stretch down one fret to F#–A# (2–6), resolving nicely to the B (V) chord, which is fully in line with the harmony previously established here.

Measure 9 begins to pick up the momentum with a recurring gallop motif on B. When E harmonic minor is played over B, we have the B Phrygian dominant scale (measure 10). After a moment hovering around F#, assisted by the chromatic addition of C# (F#'s 5th), we finally emerge on the sustaining Em–E° motif at measures 13–20.

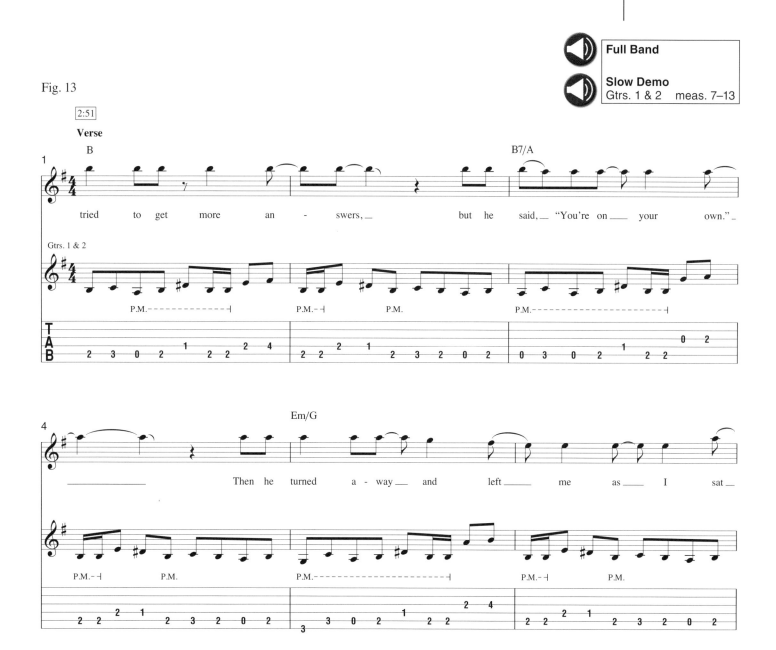

Fig. 13

Full Band

Slow Demo
Gtrs. 1 & 2   meas. 7–13

Figure 14—Guitar Solo

At 4:38, John opens the solo at high speed and builds with a repeating sextuplet pattern in the key of E minor. Alternate pick the first four notes; the last two notes of each sextuplet are pull-offs. Notice how beats 2 and 4 incorporate a string skipping pattern.

This pattern is altered in measure 2 to rise up the E natural minor scale but still maintains the same picking mechanics. This is a perfect example of the guitar "technician" side of John (using what amounts to exercise-based repetition of the sort needed to develop such high-level alternate picking skills) blended with the composer side (building the line for a greater compositional purpose, as opposed to simply showing off).

At measure 5, he slows down just a bit for a new, rhythmic motif that plays on F# and its major 7th (E#). The scale for the short fill lick that follows is F# Phrygian dominant with that major 7th added as a passing tone on the way down to E (♭7th). In harmonic terms, this lick can be regarded as F#–E#–E, falling chromatically, with Phrygian dominant decoration. Measure 6 repeats the motif but rises at the end up to a high C# (5th).

Measures 7–8 begin a single-string descending line utilizing an open B pedal. At first glance, the pattern may appear to be that of B harmonic minor. But recall that we are over F# here, so F# Phrygian dominant is the better view of things. Measure 9 gives a moment of breathing space on Em. This leads into a descending minor pentatonic box 4 shape, favoring 4th leaps via "rolling" from string to string at the seventh fret.

John comes up the Em7 arpeggio in measure 11 and then picks up the pace in measure 12. Although this is most likely the result of "cramming" the note patterns in at high speed and "floating" over the beat (coming out at the end of the phrase by feel), you can approach it for practice by playing each group of four notes as a single count in a triplet. Three sets of these (each one actually consisting of four notes) can then be played as a quarter-note triplet.

Measures 15–16 display a creative, chaotic rising effect in 16ths, whereby the notes are held steady in time (16ths), but the point at which they change feels quite random. It's a randomness that is completely intentional, of course. The odd interval leaps further add to the chaos, making heavy use of sequential 5ths and 4ths.

In measure 17, we find a descending 16th-note triplet line winding through F# Phrygian dominant. Full and dramatic six-string sweep picking takes center stage at measure 18 followed by a straight alternate picking run up E minor to cap off the phrase ending at measure 19. Notice how this run alters the E minor scale by omitting the 7th tone. This allows John to play a sextuplet using exactly the same scale tones in each octave, on each successive beat, and rise quickly through three full octaves in just three beats.

John goes glam metal pentatonic soloing in measure 20 over F#, using pentatonic box 1. But as usual, this only lasts for a brief moment—just enough to send a "familiar feel" and pull the listener in before quickly taking us into more unusual territory. At measure 21, the keys join in for a descending sequenced run that begins in F# minor pentatonic box 2 and turns diminished. Measure 22 repeats 21 down an octave.

Fig. 14

4:38

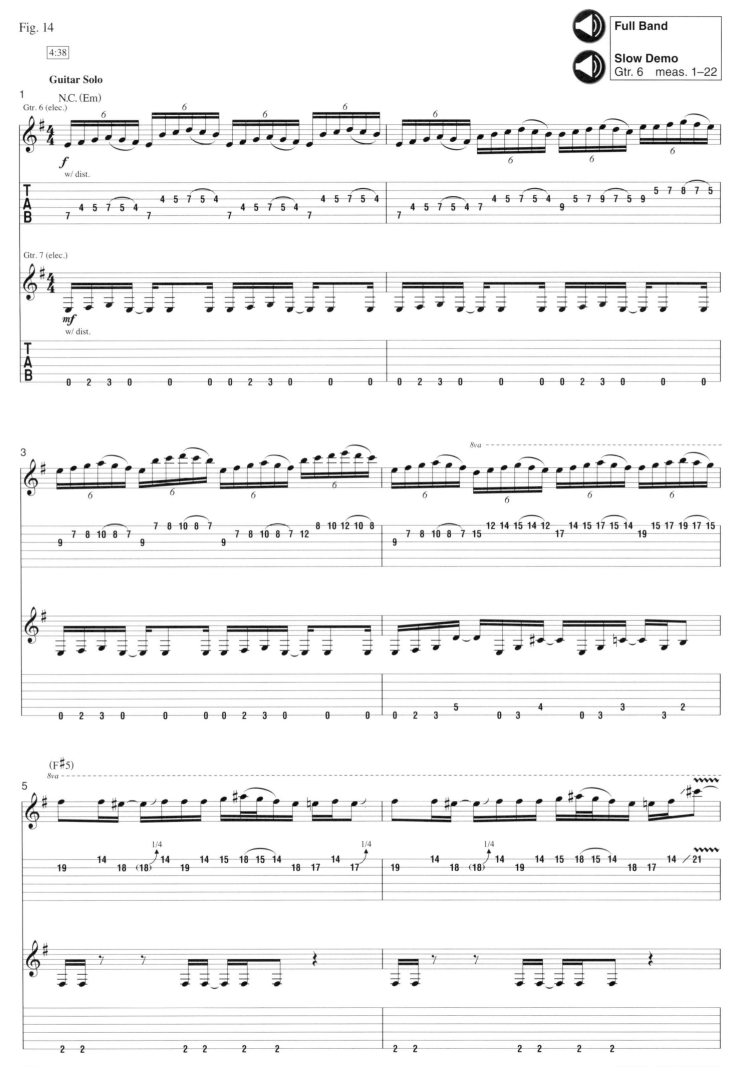

FATAL TRAGEDY

HOME

(*Metropolis, Pt. 2: Scenes from a Memory*, 1999)

Music by John Petrucci, John Myung, Jordan Rudess, James LaBrie and Mike Portnoy
Lyrics by Mike Portnoy

"Home" is track 8 on the *Metropolis, Pt. 2: Scenes from a Memory* album and opens Act 2. The tuning for Gtrs. 1–5 is drop D, whereby strings 1–5 remain in standard tuning and the low sixth string is dropped a full step from E down to D.

Figure 15—Intro

The soundscape introduction initially features Eastern instruments and motifs. Heavy guitar then breaks in at 1:44 with a simplified version of the same tonality. A strong emphasis on the opening low D eighth notes is created by virtue of a wah-wah pedal effect punching them at the start of every one-measure riff. Also notice the hemiola (three against two) rhythmic pattern in the riff throughout beats 2, 3, and 4 within the 16ths. This is characteristic of the type of rhythmic displacement we find in many metal riffs as a means to add rhythmic interest.

The key signature of two flats (Bb–Eb) in this case indicates the modal tonality of D Phrygian (D–Eb–F–G–A–Bb–C), although at both the beginning soundscape and also later as the riff evolves at measure 4, we find that the full scale is really that of D Phrygian dominant (D–Eb–F#–G–A–Bb–C)—the difference being the major 3rd within Phrygian dominant (F#), which lends a characteristic and dramatic brightness to the scale, as opposed to the darker minor 3rd of Phrygian. The F therefore is sharped using accidentals within the staff. Phrygian dominant is also known as the Spanish Gypsy or Spanish Flamenco scale.

At measure 5, John adds an evocative melody line that further draws upon the exotic sound of the scale, with added Eastern-sounding articulations in the form of grace-note downward slides into the major 3rds (F#). Gtr. 3 doubles the melody an octave higher, but the lower octave of the melody (Gtr. 4) is far more prominent.

Contrast comes at measure 13, as all the fanfare comes to an abrupt halt, and a new riff enters—a crushing and menacing, yet very simple and totally effective in the best metal fashion, D5 palm mute. One-finger power chord slides fill the end of measure 14. First we have A5–Bb5 (5–b6), identifying the key as that of D minor. Then we hear G5–Ab5 (4–b5), hanging for a moment on the tritone, which gives us a characteristic, twisted metal feel. The ending at measure 16 swaps in a different single-note fill drawn from the D Phrygian scale. This becomes the central figure for the verse that follows.

Fig. 15

Gtrs. 1–5, Drop D tuning:
(low to high) D-A-D-G-B-E

1:44

Intro
Moderately ♩ = 90

*Doubled throughout

Gtrs. 1 & 2 tacet

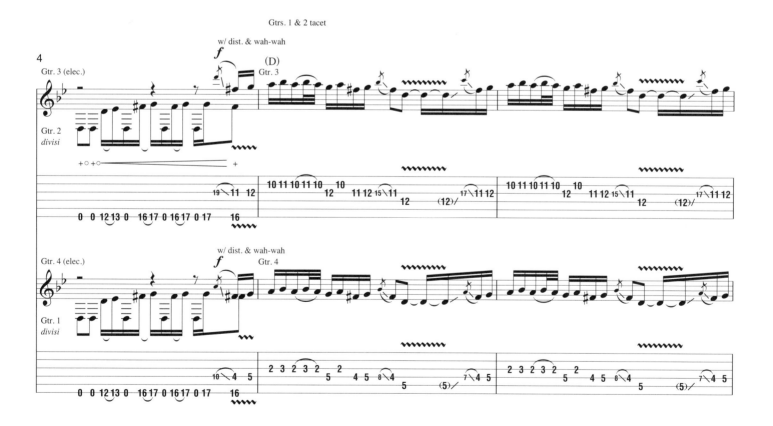

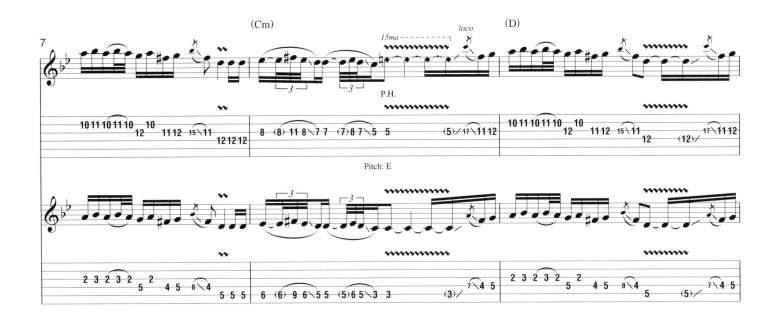

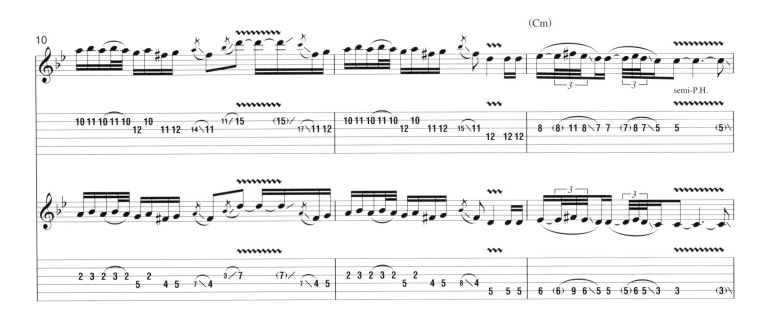

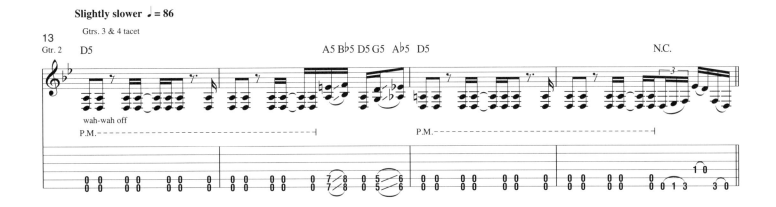

Figure 16—Pre-Chorus, Interlude

While the song is in D minor overall, at the title hook lyric, "home," we temporarily shift up to G minor (iv). Rather than chording, however, John opts to texture this section with a palm-muted single-note line. Measure 2 begins to repeat the first-measure pattern until beat 3, when it rises up the D minor scale utilizing the tones 4–5–♭6, 1–2–♭3, and 5–♭6.

Next we move up to A (V) for two measures. Open A eighth notes on beat 1 mirror the earlier D5 riff motif. But here John is busy, filling the entire two measures. The scale is A Phrygian dominant, which, being the fifth mode of harmonic minor, uses the same notes as D harmonic minor, but of course here A (V) is the temporary chord tone "base." Notice the 6th intervals on beat 2. The shape 5–7 on strings 6 and 5, which form a power chord shape in standard tuning, are now that of a major 6th in drop D tuning. The next interval is a minor 6th. The following two intervals are minor 6ths. All arise from A Phrygian dominant. Measures 5–6 return to Gm (iv) as before, except this time John vaults into a sextuplet run at the end, building into the blazing section that follows.

Perhaps the strongest sonic impact at the interlude/solo section is due to an abrupt and unexpected key change, which causes the mood to shift noticeably. The chords Ab–Fm set up and drop into the chorus that follows in C minor, which is down a whole step from the D minor that the song has been in thus far. Seen from the perspective of the new key of C minor, Ab–Fm–Cm is a ♭VI–iv–i progression. Yet Ab is also the tritone (♭V) relative to the old key of D minor. So the abrupt shift to Ab sounds at once very odd and yet also quite bright, as it is a strong major chord in the C minor progression.

The run is in straight C natural minor. Mechanically, we see a 16-note sequence that fills up two full beats of 32nd notes on strings 3 and 4. The pattern winds around in a somewhat circular manner and completes itself on the higher string. In the next two beats, we see the same pattern repeat on string pair 2–3, albeit now conforming to the pattern of the C minor scale on those two strings. Use straight alternate picking.

At measure 8, John begins a third repetition of the same gradually ascending sequence on string pair 1–2. But this gives way to a new method of ascent—upward position shifts with downward note motion in each shift. At beat 3, John breaks that pattern for a longer diatonic run. He closes with a quick middle finger position shift up to the final descending line, to end on the root, C, at the start of the chorus.

Full Band

Slow Demo
Gtr. 5   meas. 7–9

Fig. 16

3:45

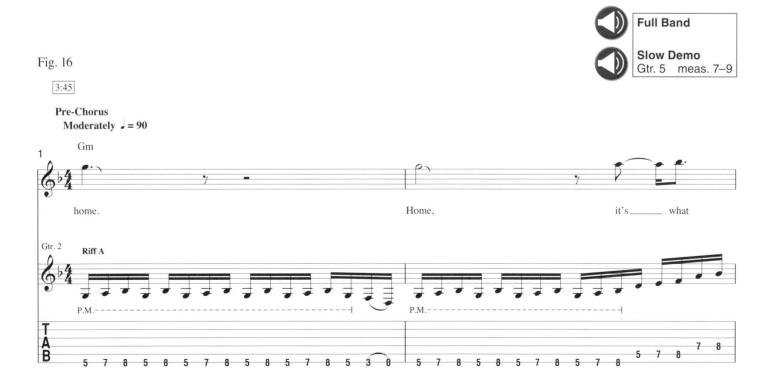

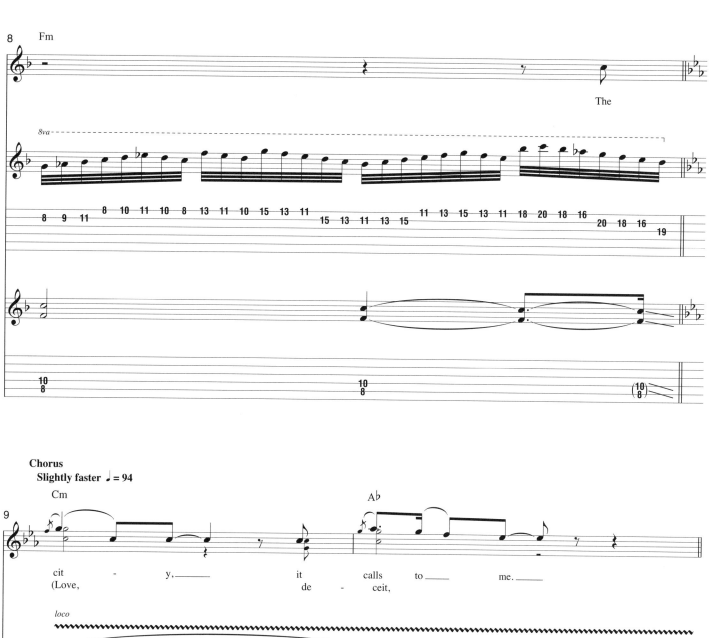

Figure 17—Guitar Solo

In the storyline, the character Victoria is leaving Julian due to his addictions and finds some comfort crying on the shoulder of Julian's brother, Edward. Edward, after some internal wrestling with his own sense of impropriety, falls for her nonetheless and eventually becomes obsessed. He seduces her, and the music falls to a low ebb, as the Eastern instrumentation we first heard at the start of the song takes over (7:30). The energy builds as we hear Victoria's moans beginning softly around 8:00 and rising. The keyboard solo takes over and builds the energy further, first over Gm and then back to the central intro riff in D Phrygian. Lastly, the 28-measure guitar solo enters on the heels of the keyboard, full of slinky, exotic, Eastern-sounding motifs and articulations. John builds it gradually, drawing out the extended interlude for roughly a full minute. It's not the first time a guitar solo would be presented as the musical expression of love-making (think Led Zeppelin "Whole Lotta Love" solo); nevertheless, it is possibly the first to set such a thing within the larger framework of a concept album storyline, and John pulls it off flawlessly.

First, over G, he opens with a strong pull-off to sound the open G string, while simultaneously dropping the whammy bar to nearly slack and then pulling it up gradually. The scale is G Phrygian dominant for six measures. Notice the strong tension created by F♯ (7th) at the end of measure 3 and again at the beginning of measure 6. A Phrygian dominant with a raised (major) 7th is also known as the double harmonic scale. This is because the tones 5–♭6–7–8, found in the harmonic minor scale, contain a characteristic feature of a minor 3rd interval sandwiched in between half steps. This same feature occurs between tones 1–♭2–3–4 of the Phrygian dominant scale. So, in essence the "double harmonic" scale is so named because it uniquely contains two of these unique structures.

At the end of eight measures over G (IV), we see a nice 32nd-note run played exclusively on the first string and used as a pickup into the A (V) section that comes next. Pay special attention to making the position shifts smooth so that they sound seamless. Moving up to the dominant (V) for measures 9–16 sustains the energy at an even higher level. Here, the predominant scale is A Phrygian dominant (and double harmonic with the appearance of G♯, the major 7th). Measures 9–10 feature rhythmically displaced motifs with Eastern-style downward slide articulations. At measures 11–14, the phrasing gets a little busier rhythmically, yet John is still dancing around the scale, not quite going full tilt. It's not until measure 15 that he finally builds into a straight 32nd-note line. Notice how John applies the A Phrygian dominant scale; he keeps the pattern mechanical by using three-note-per-string shapes, but, by virtue of skipping occasional tones of the scale, he ascends somewhat diagonally rather than moving straight across the neck in the standard three-note-per-string shapes. Doing this enables the run to span a greater range of pitch without any large position shifts; there are a few smaller shifts instead, which are much easier to manage seamlessly.

At measure 17, the underlying chord moves back to G, but this time it's Gm, and the riff is actually what was played at the pre-chorus. In the solo, John slows a bit and waxes melodic, now applying G natural minor and flowing into G minor pentatonic and blues at the end of measure 18. Measures 19–20 are over A. John uses a "backwards" sequenced two-note pattern to ascend, double picking each note and transforming 16ths into 32nds.

Still in lock step with the pre-chorus progression, measures 21–22 return to Gm. Although some may prefer economy picking for the sextuplets, use strict alternate picking here to achieve true Petrucci "evenness" of execution. Measures 23 and 24 are over A♭–Fm and use the same diatonic C natural minor approach as we saw earlier in the pre-chorus.

Fig. 17

Full Band

Slow Demo
Gtr. 6   meas. 8–25

9:21

Guitar Solo

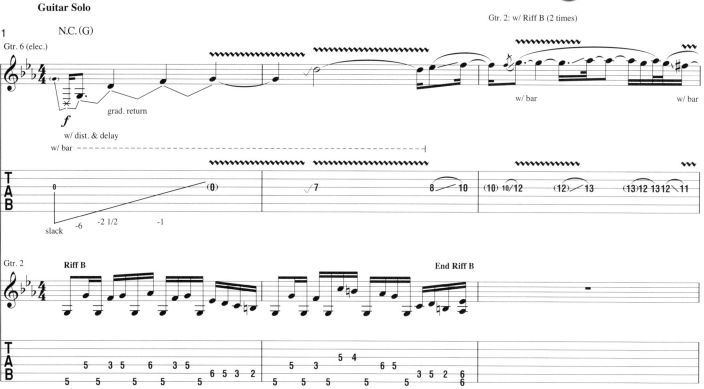

Gtr. 2: w/ Riff B (2 times)

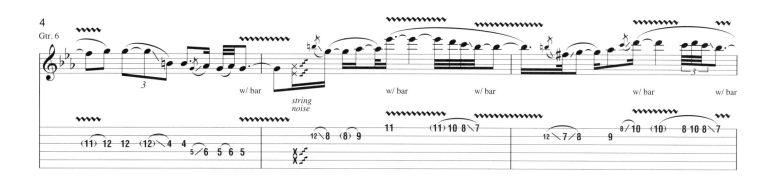

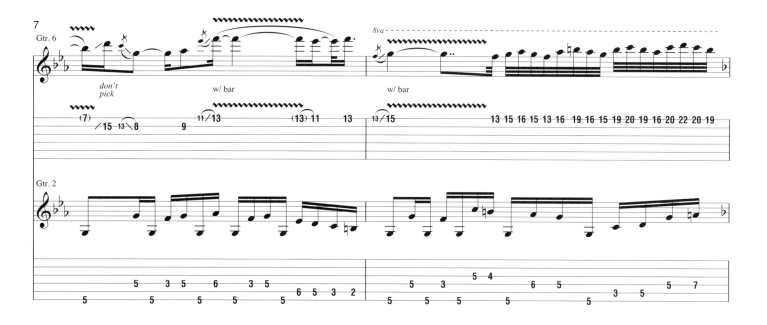

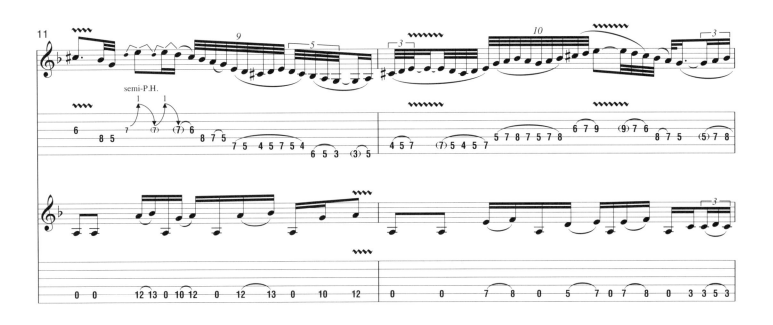

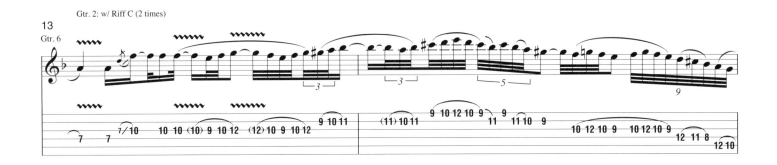

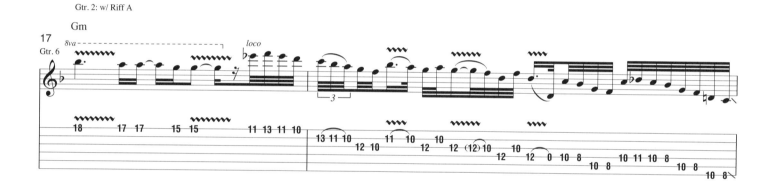

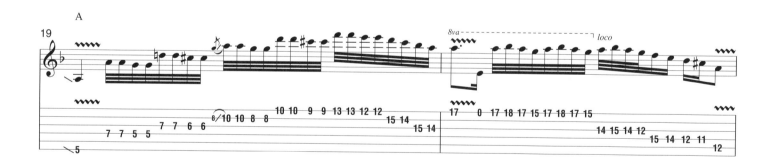

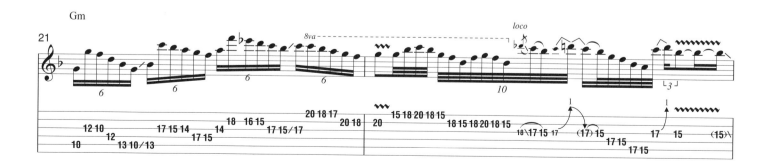

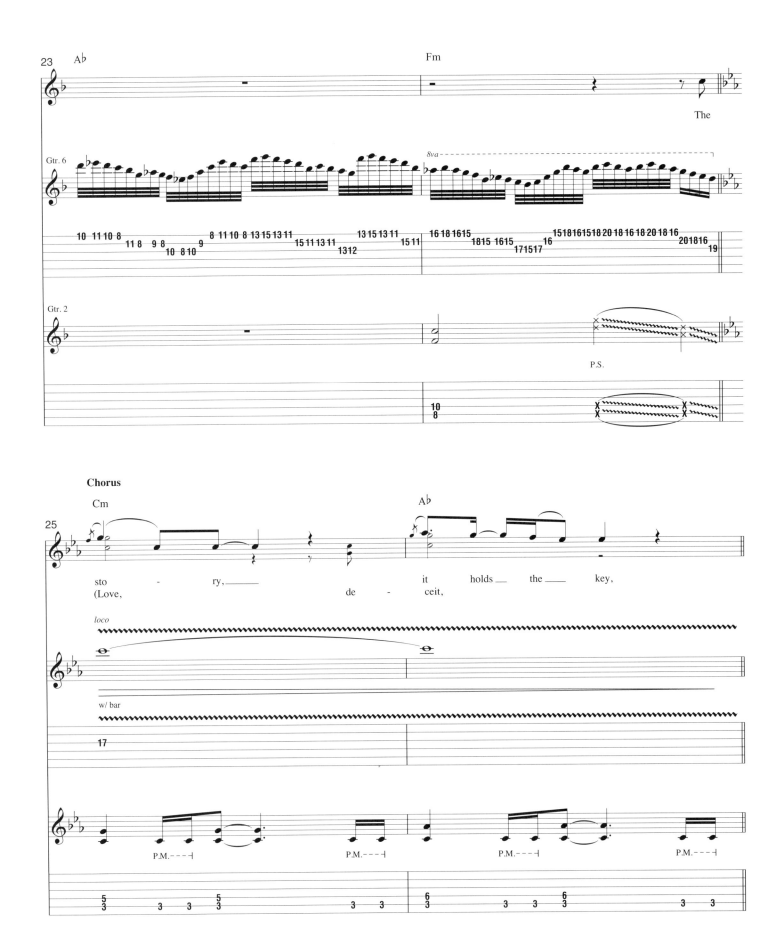

THE GLASS PRISON

(*Six Degrees of Inner Turbulence*, 2002)

**Music by John Myung, John Petrucci, Michael Portnoy
and Jordan Rudess
Words by Michael Portnoy**

Six Degrees of Inner Turbulence, released in 2002, is a concept album exploring the themes of life struggle such as addiction, isolation, loss of faith, and the sanctity of life and death. The first song on the album, "The Glass Prison," is also the beginning of the Twelve-Step Suite—a series of songs written by Portnoy, beginning with *Six Degrees of Inner Turbulence* and continuing through *Black Clouds & Silver Linings*, about his experience in rehabilitation from alcoholism. The twelve steps are, of course, the twelve steps of Alcoholics Anonymous. As the first song in the Suite, "The Glass Prison" is composed in three parts, written to mirror the first three steps of AA. Although spread across multiple albums, the band did in fact compose these pieces with the intention of eventually playing it live as one piece.

Figure 18—Intro

The track opens with white noise—perhaps the "noise" in Portnoy's head. The music begins innocently but becomes crushingly brutal soon enough. By 1:44, the sense of desperation is palpable. The heavy, driving riffing seems an apt representation of life closing in, as the coping mechanism of the past no longer provides relief but only serves to make matters worse, and the vicious cycle of alcoholism hits full swing. At 2:22, the lead guitar enters with a fantastically crazy series of classically inspired arpeggios over the low B pedal tone, portraying the insanity, with seemingly no way out.

Pay attention to the indicated alternate picking approach, whereby you skip the upstroke for the pull-off but otherwise maintain the rhythmically determined alternate picking throughout. This is no small feat when performing 16th notes at 170 bpm. Be sure to minimize the distance your pick travels as well as the level of tension in your picking hand.

The first arpeggio is Bm, followed by A#°7. Instead of resolving back to Bm, however, the diminished 7th falls a half step to A°7 (or D#°7 if you want to name it according to standard classical practice, as it resolves to Em). Alternatively, if you view each chord as simply an extended version of its single leading note—the other pitches of each arpeggio being essentially added "harmony," if you will—you can see a melody by looking at just the leading pitches: B–A#–A–G. When we do this, we see a descending line with chromaticism.

At measure 4, we have the leading note E# (within C#7), which is the #4th relative to the pedal tone B. And the #4th pulls strongly up to 5th, F#, which is the first tone of the following Bm arpeggio at measure 5, kicking off the next portion of the phrase.

At measure 5, the F# (5th) falls a half step to F natural and then E in measure 6, mirroring the motif established earlier in measures 1–2. This resolves to G at measure 7 and then A at the shortened 2/4 measure, again as a mirror to the previous 2/4 measure 4. So the entire eight-measure series of beginning notes is: B–A#–A–G, then F#–F–E–D.

Measure 9 moves to Dm, both in the rhythm line and in the lead. Since D is actually the relative major of B minor, it is quite closely related. However, instead of staying true to the key and using D major, John shifts into the parallel minor tonality (D minor), which is to say he is swapping out a minor harmony where our ears would expect to hear major. Measures 9–12 and 13–16 echo the first eight-measure motif, except this time around D minor.

Measures 17–24 move the key center to C# minor (ii relative to the original key of B minor) for a third repetition of the motif, shifted to yet another pitch. This time, the shortened final 2/4 measure dispenses with arpeggios and instead features a rising chromatic line leading up toward B, at the start of measure 25.

At measure 25, we hear a new 6/4 riff on the low B string. The tonality of the riff is B Phrygian/blues: a Phrygian mode with the added ♭5th of the blues scale. These tones are peppered against a low B palm-muted pedal tone with syncopated eighth-note rhythms in proper down-tuned metal fashion.

Full Band

Slow Demo
Gtr. 3   meas. 1–25

Fig. 18

All gtrs. 7-string elec.

Intro
Moderately fast ♩ = 170

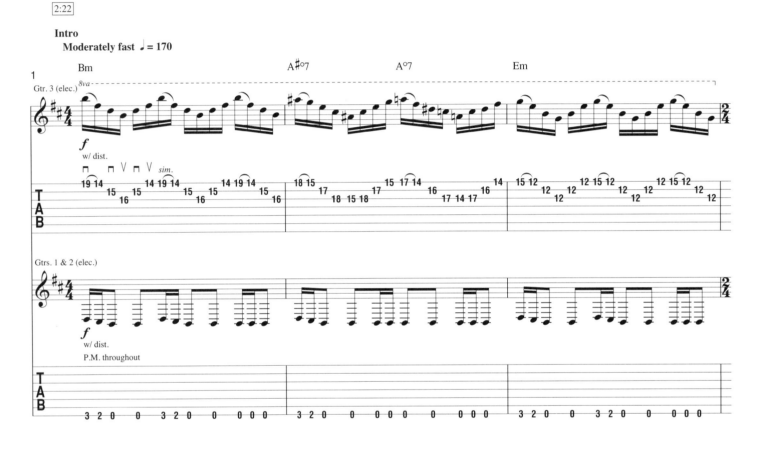

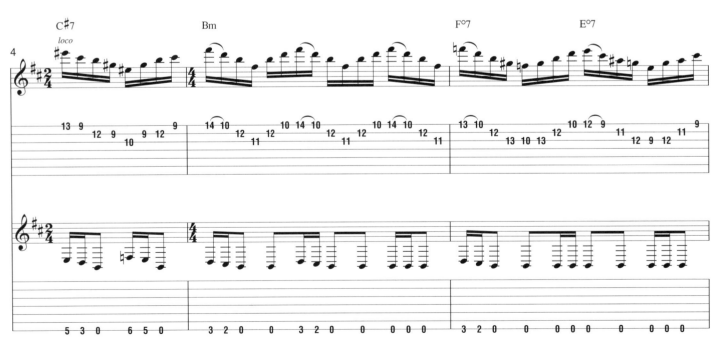

THE GLASS PRISON

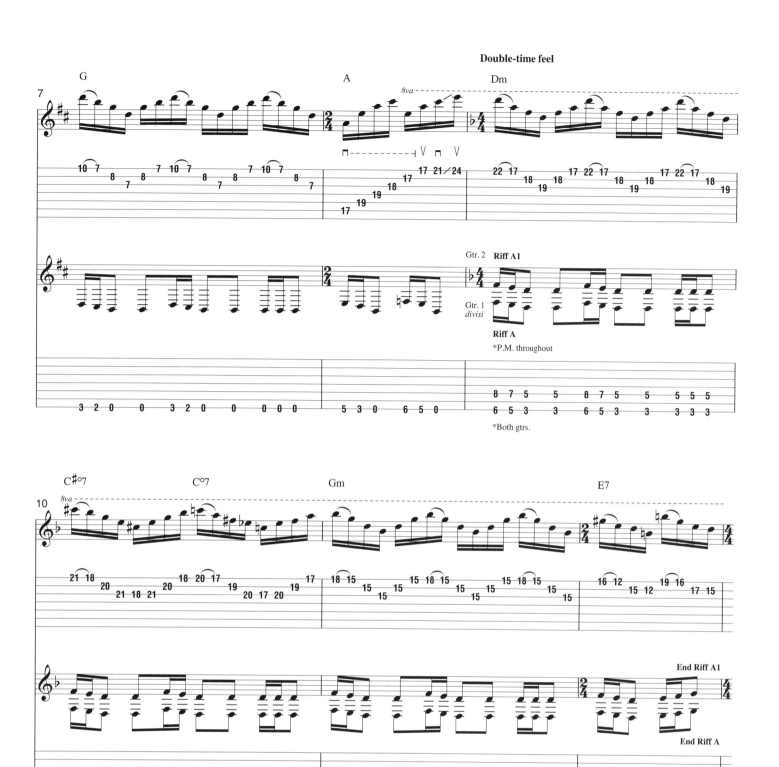

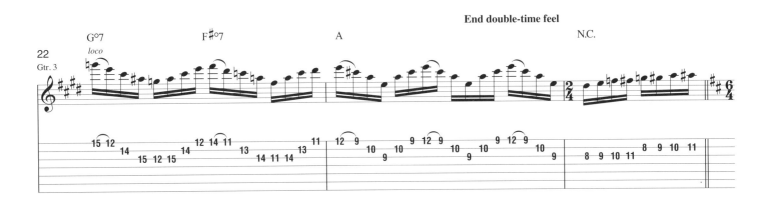

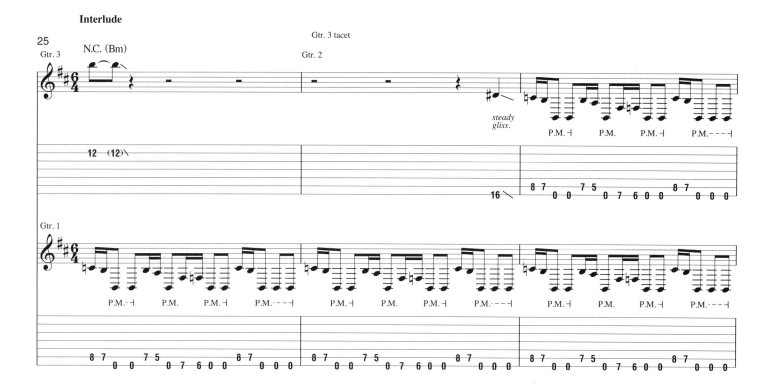

Figure 19—Chorus

The chorus texture is dominated by a half-time drum feel, while on guitar an open B string rings throughout above a moving lower voice. The effect of this compositionally is to seem to spread the music out "wide" (as opposed to the narrower "front and center" quality of driving riffs), which thereby allows the instrumentation to seemingly duck behind the vocal lyric and portray a "breathing space"—i.e., a feeling of relief and withdrawal from the stresses of the world. This is Portnoy's "comfort zone," courtesy of his friend alcohol. But of course, just as alcohol serves his emotional need to retreat, this benefit is one for which he must pay dearly, as it also enslaves him and has begun to destroy him.

Technically speaking, measure 1 has F# in the bass, creating a Bm/F# (second inversion Bm). When the bass note rises to A (♭7th) at beat 4, the composite tonality of the measure becomes Bm7. At the start of measure 2, notice how the sustaining open B string eighth-note motif now hits on beat 1—a rhythmic displacement technique at work, since in the first measure it appeared on beat 2, which is where we might more naturally expect it to recur. Measure 3 repeats measure 1, so the open string now hits on beat 2. Then, to complete the phrase, measure 4 ducks down to E5, which is the IV chord relative to the key center of B, creating a i–IV motion. The next four measures are similar but end on D5, creating a i–♭III progression.

This entire eight-measure pattern then repeats but for a change in fills. At measure 12, we see natural harmonics employed, outlining the tones of E major. Then we see something very odd at measure 16…

Normally, as phrases go, we experience musical time expecting some degree of parity. That is, after one idea, we expect a counterbalancing idea, or "answer." So after one motif, perhaps, we hear the idea repeated differently. It's common to return to the starting point and then perhaps fill the remainder of the phrase differently. But the entire phrase is universally made up of even lengths—two, four, eight, 16. On, off, back and forth, question and answer, call and response. However, when extra time is added or withdrawn from the phrase, it throws a curve at us.

So here at measure 16, we are naturally anticipating that this measure must complete the fourth four-measure phrase. Then we will be ready to hear a new four-measure phrase begin at measure 17. Instead, Dream Theater cut out an entire bar, and the whole band modulates up (changes keys) unexpectedly and starts the chorus again, before we are ready. Before, we saw a similar technique occur by virtue of dropping out a beat or a single eighth note here and there (introducing odd time signatures). In this case, the same idea is being applied on a larger level of phrase length.

Dream Theater also punch up the unexpectedness of this even more by playing beat 1 of measure 16 on D—so they begin measure 16 exactly as we would expect—with a repetition of the Bm–D (i–IV) progression. Then a modulation occurs on beat 2 and the lyrics begin the chorus instantly on beat 2. We are left scratching our heads, wondering how we got to the new key and where exactly the change occurred. This, of course, is possible here because the chorus lyric actually starts on beat 2. Very tricky…

Fig. 19 **Full Band**

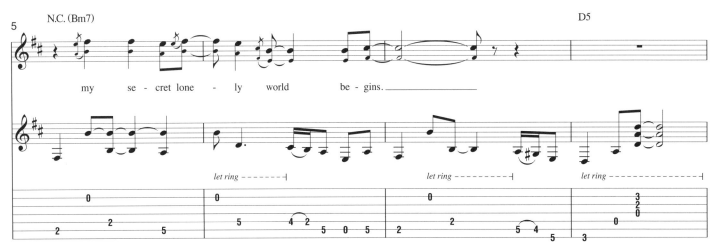

THE GLASS PRISON

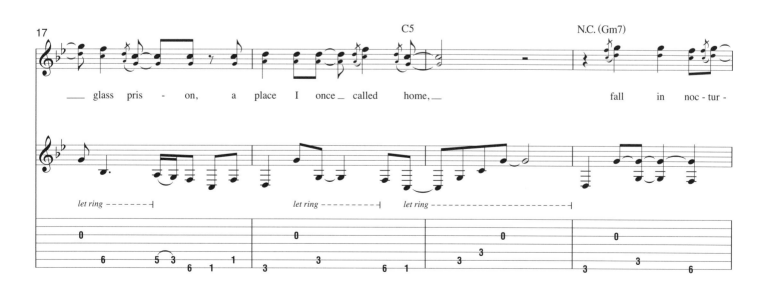

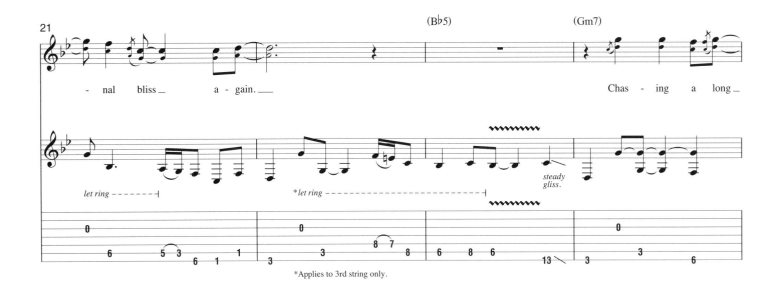

*Applies to 3rd string only.

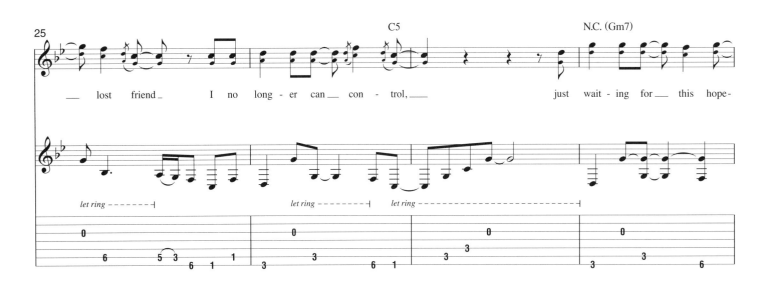

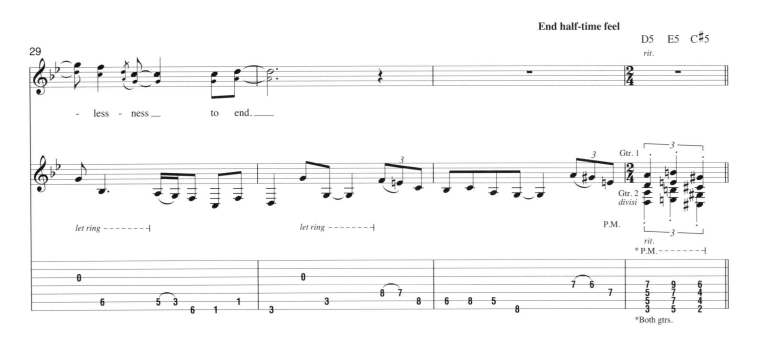

*Both gtrs.

Figure 20—Guitar Solo, Keyboard Solo, Guitar/Keyboard Unison, Interlude

At 10:25, John launches the guitar solo with a repeating, cyclic pattern in sextuplets. This consists of E–F#–G–B–G–F# (4–5–♭6–1–♭6–5) drawn from B natural minor. At 144 bpm, this is a great speed exercise. After two measures, he alters the pattern to shift first down and back up via position shifting. Use finger 1 for the first fret 14–12 shift, then use finger 2 and 1 to play the next fret 14 and 12. Next, shift your first finger down to fret 10, and use finger 3 to play fret 12 on the first note of beat 2.

The fingering for the six notes on beat 2 is then 3–1–1–3–1–1. And beat 3 is 2–1–1–3–1–1. After that, you should get the idea for how to approach the rest of the phrase.

Measure 5 starts a new arpeggiated idea with a rhythmically displaced motif. That is, the motif is six notes long, and when repeated in 16th notes, the repetition falls differently against the pulse. Where the motif first started on a downbeat, it now starts on an upbeat. Since the higher notes in particular stand out from the pattern, this rhythmic displacement has the effect of shifting those accent points to create interesting syncopations. At measure 7, John begins a repetition of the arpeggiated motif but twists it into a chromatic ascent. Three-string sweep technique completes the phrase in measure 8.

The keyboard solo takes over for eight measures, as if challenging the lead guitar (a challenge no keyboardist can ever really win regardless of his or her skill level—as we know, it simply can't be done). At this point, the guitar moves into a supporting ostinato role, as straight 16ths vamp on F# minor pentatonic, harmonically.

At measure 14, however, we see the challenge is all in good fun, as keyboard and guitar now join together in unison back on B minor pentatonic. Measure 14 is a classical pedal tone idea, coming down B natural minor. The repeated pedal tone is on top in this case—first D (♭3rd) and then B (root).

Measure 17 rips quickly down B minor pentatonic box 2 in sextuplets. This is deceptively difficult to perform at this speed, as two-note-per-string patterns cover a lot more distance than the same speed of notes played in the diatonic, three-note-per-string patterns. John shifts up into box 3 and then 4 in measures 18–20. Measure 21 shifts the motif up an octave into the top of B minor pentatonic box 5.

A breakdown interlude occurs at measures 22–25 with clean guitar and keyboard harmony. Such abrupt changes of tone and texture are one of John's trademarks, striving to use the full range of contrast available for maximum compositional variety.

Fig. 20

Full Band

Slow Demo
Gtr. 3   meas. 1–8,
14–22

THE GLASS PRISON

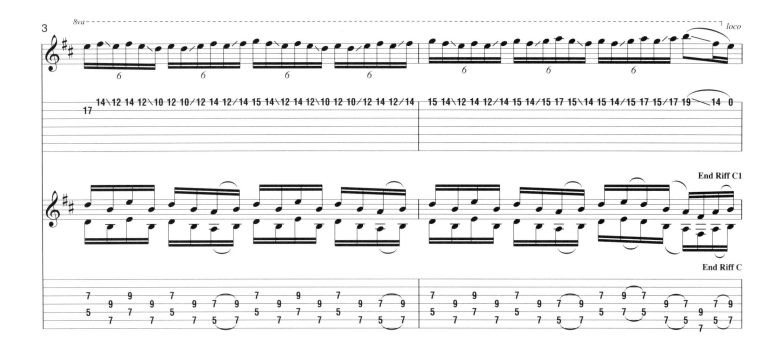

Gtr. 1: w/ Riff C (1st 2 meas.)
Gtr. 2: w/ Riff C1 (1st 2 meas.)

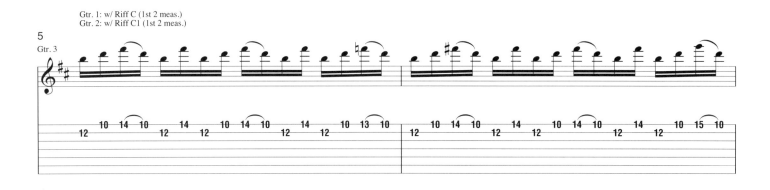

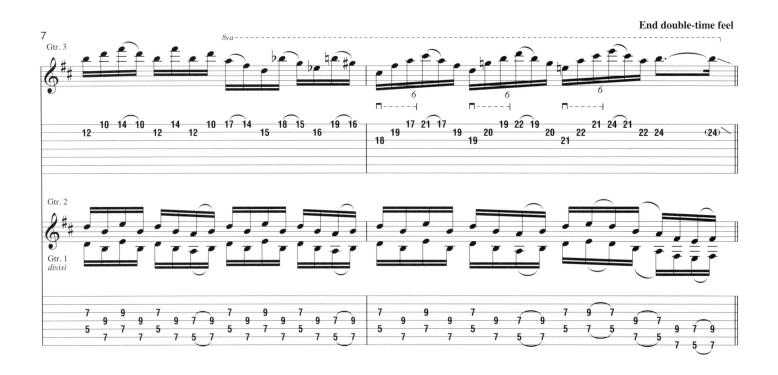

THE GLASS PRISON

Keyboard Solo

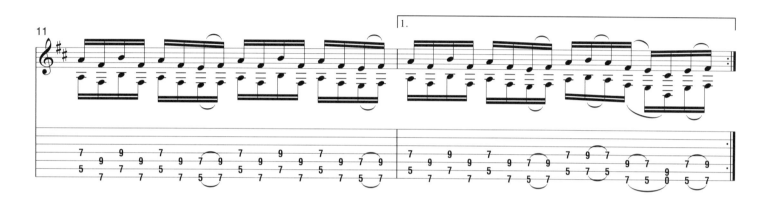

Guitar & Keyboard Unison

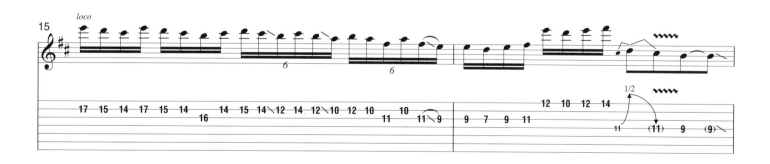

Interlude

N.C.(Em)

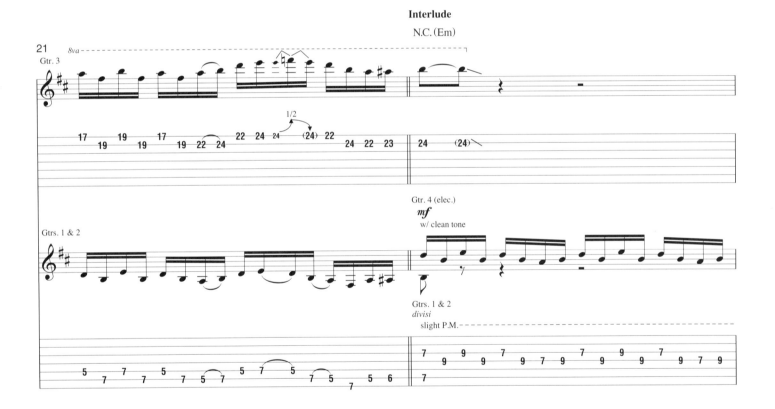

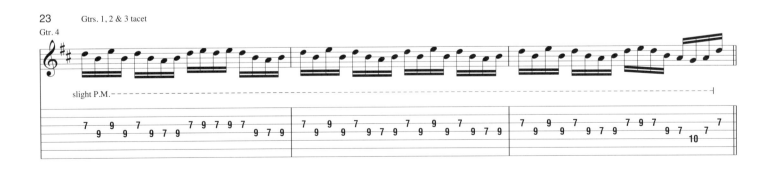

ENDLESS SACRIFICE

(*Train of Thought*, 2003)

Music by John Petrucci, John Myung, Jordan Rudess and Mike Portnoy
Lyrics by John Petrucci

With the enthusiastic live audience response to the band's heavier songs, Dream Theater chose to go heavier and darker with *Train of Thought*, the seventh studio album. In the "Chaos in Progress" documentary video, Portnoy says they wanted it to be "balls to the wall" and bring in new metal fans. This effort is clearly evident in the song "Endless Sacrifice."

First, notice that the tuning is down a whole step across the board. This means that the actual sounding pitches of the open strings are, from low to high: D–G–C–F–A–D. However, as is standard practice with slack tunings, we notate the staff and chord symbols using the pitches as if they were still in standard tuning—the low sixth string is still written and referred to as "E"—but with the caveat that the actual sounding pitch of everything will be a full step lower due to the tuning.

Figure 21—Intro

The song opens with an arpeggiated clean guitar line in E minor. The short two-measure motif features an added 9th tone (F♯) and prominent minor 3rd via the sustaining open G string. John plays with the minor 6th/major 6th as he so often does in measure 2, then abruptly closes on B (V). The second time, in measures 3–4, he substitutes the more common G, creating a more cliché Em–C–G progression (i–♭VI–♭III). However, notice the added Dream Theater-ism at measure 5; an extra two beats are tacked on, to make things somewhat unexpected.

Measures 6–9 repeat the general idea, although we see that Dadd4 replaces the C♯° and B5 at the end of measure 7. Dadd4 is created by virtue of inserting the open G common tone over D. Finally, in another characteristic phrasing "obfuscation" move, the band adds another partial measure to cap off the phrase. But instead of adding two beats as previously—that may now become exactly what you might expect—this time they add three, to keep us guessing.

Fig. 21

Tune down 1 step:
(low to high) D-G-C-F-A-D

0:25

Intro
Moderately slow ♩ = 87

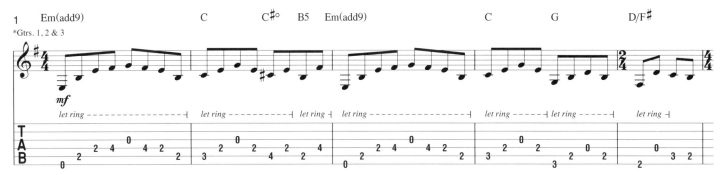

*Gtr. 1 (acous.);
Gtr. 2 (elec.) w/ clean tone;
Gtr. 3 (elec.) w/ clean tone & piezo pickup

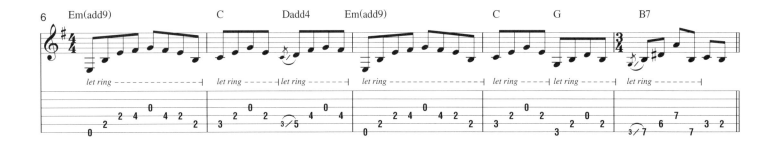

Figure 22—Pre-Chorus, Chorus

At the start of the pre-chorus at 1:42, the song modulates into and begins to revolve around A minor (which is the iv chord relative to the original key of E minor). Now the progression is Am–F#°–F, then Am–Dm–E7. Next, we have yet another shifty pulse fakeout, but this time only one extra beat is added. Rather than write a 1/4 measure, however, here the notation simply transforms the preceding measure into 5/4. After this, we repeat the core, four-measure progression once again. To close the pre-chorus, we see the "extra beat" idea inserted for the fourth time, now as the length of a full four-beat measure (measure 9).

The chorus turns heavy and kicks into overdrive with a straight-up nu metal style riff. Rhythmic displacement and timed natural harmonic "screeches" dominate the character here. Basically, after E5 punches on beat 1, we have a motif consisting of an E palm mute pickup, followed by a G5–A5 slide and final E5 punch. This motif is then repeated and displaced 180° against the pulse, causing downbeats to become upbeats and upbeats to become downbeats. The E5 pedal point accents form the rhythmic pattern of downbeat 1, upbeat 2, downbeat 4. A natural harmonic at fret 4, string 3 sounds a high B note (5th) in the hole on upbeat 4.

Measure 11 begins the same but uses an alternate ending on beat 4, with B5–F#5 (5–2) power chords on eighth notes. Measures 12–13 repeat this but with a different ending—16th palm mutes on C5 and D5. This standard "alternate ending" approach to metal riff form can be represented here as ABAC; in this case "A" would represent the main riff with the harmonic ending (measures 10 and 12), "B" would represent the riff with the eighth-note power chord ending (measure 11), and "C" would represent the riff with the final 16th palm mute ending (measure 13).

Finally, notice that the title lyric hook actually enters in the final measure 17 and continues right into the interlude that follows. Compositionally, this phrasing technique weaves these sections together and steps beyond the standard and more typical approach of completing the chorus *within* its eight-measure allotment.

Fig. 22

Full Band

1:42

Pre-Chorus

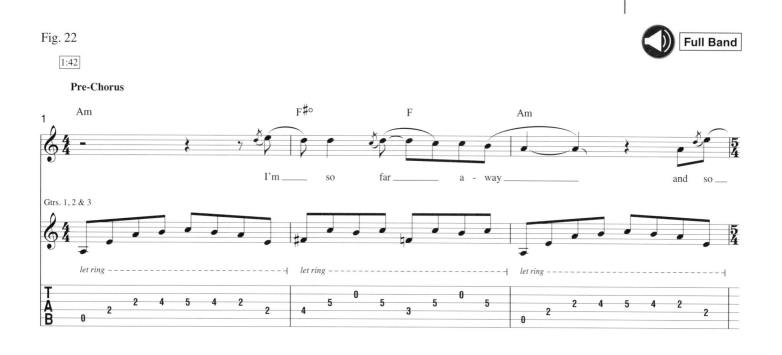

Chorus

Moderately slow ♩ = 90

Gtrs. 1, 2 & 3 tacet

Try ___ to stay a - live ___ un - til I hear your voice. I'm ___ gon-na lose my mind.

*Gtr. 4 (elec.)

*Doubled throughout

Some - one ___ tell ___ me why ___ I chose this life, ___ this su - per - fi - cial lie.

Interlude

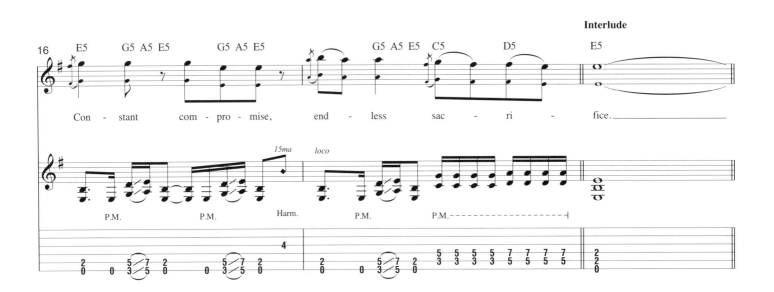

Con - stant com - pro - mise, end - less sac - ri - fice. ___

Figure 23—Interlude

The interlude at 5:43 begins firmly planted in progressive rock and then shifts into experimental/fusion territory before finally coming back to straight-up metal roots. Defining a temporary key center of A minor, John skirts between major and minor 6th (F#–F) and winds around to C (♭III) in the two-measure phrase of straight eighth notes. Rhythmically, the standout motif consists of a two-note interval jump on beats 1 (A–E, a 5th) and 3 (F#–D, a minor 6th). John throws us a curve by omitting the low note at the start of measure 2 and instead jabs right at the upper C, a 5th above the preceding F. But as F–C clearly sets up a similar parallel idea, pitch-wise, this makes the accent point on C at downbeat 1 all the more unexpected. (We might expect to hear E–C.) At the slide into D, shift positions to use your first finger, then second and third, for the chromatic ascent. The last three pitches (E–G–C) are all found within C major (♭III).

At measures 3–4, the phrase repeats, more or less, with a few alterations. First, we jump up an octave. Second, we drop an eighth note out of the first measure, just to mess up the timing that much more—a Dream Theater trademark. Third, we get downright crazy in measure 4. Ascending tritones spell out D#° (or B7 if you like), which pull to an arpeggiated E chord at the notes B–E (5–1), followed by a leap down to low E as if to underscore it as the target. But just as quickly, we walk up to B (5th) via F (♭2nd) to add another melodic tritone element. The speed of the notes is moderate here—slow enough to allow the oddity of the pitches to sink in, but fast enough that it's almost hard to follow at first listen.

At measures 9–12, things get even stranger. Now the 7/8 measure leads, while the notes walk up in a distinct pattern using 6ths. The last beat of every other measure now features a distinct syncopated 16th jab. Measures 13–16 repeat the previous four-measure phrase without palm muting.

The section appearing at measures 17–22 is the full-on experimental portion. John ascends chromatically with interspersed arpeggiated tritones, and the timing gets even more bizarre and whimsical. An 11/8 measure signals six beats with a missing half beat. Measure 18 combines the tritone ascent with the syncopated jab motif from just before but with full stops on the rest, making the rhythm feel completely arbitrary.

Descending at measures 20–21, we have what appears to be a B♭+add9 with chromaticism followed by A♭+add9—weird tone combinations. Then at measure 22, we have a set of three triplets on descending augmented arpeggios, planting a decidedly "lost" sensation like falling through clouds, perhaps. This falls chromatically to F# and, finally, we return to something a bit more "solid."

At measure 23, we return to the land of rock for an F#m Phrygian/blues riff. This is contrasted, however, at the end of measures 24 and 26 with quick major 3rd (A#) stabs. Finally, at measure 27, we drop to the lower octave to restate the riff in a more serious, metallic fashion. Here, power chords are added to the accent points.

Fig. 23

5:43

Full Band

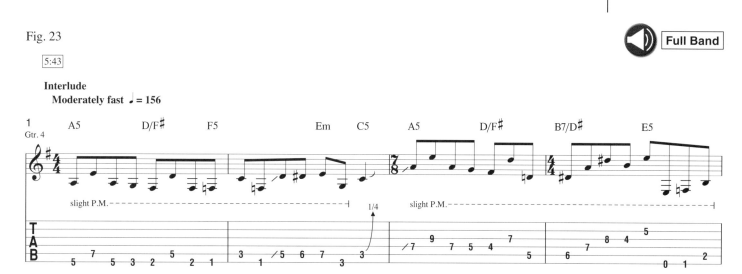

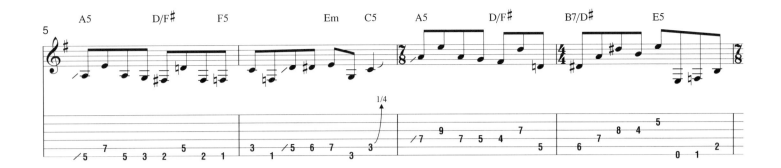

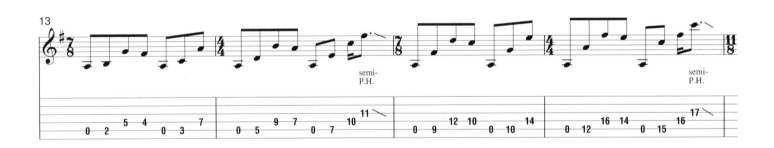

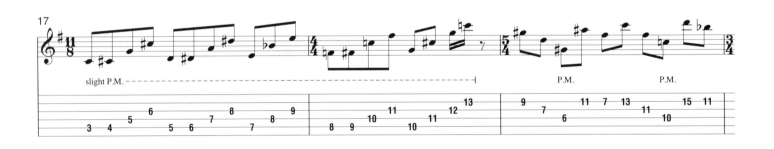

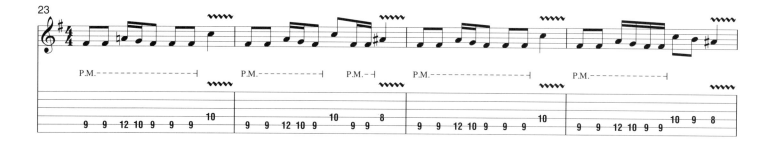

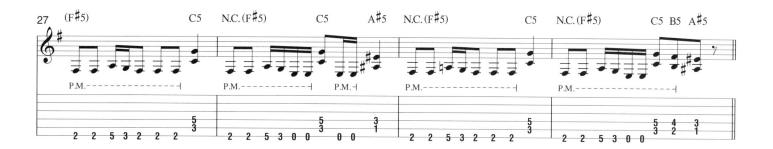

Figure 24—Guitar Solo

The solo opens with a four-measure line of alternate picked 16th notes in the E blues scale (E–G–A–B♭–B–D) omitting the 4th (A). The line is built from a repeated six-note pattern, played four times and with an alternating bass pedal point (G–E) as the lowest pitch. The fifth time, John leaves the motif behind and rises higher, utilizing an E minor pentatonic shape that includes the same pitch (D) on both the second and third strings. At measure 3, he descends the pattern using a two-note sequence that turns diatonic roughly halfway to its conclusion on F♯ (2nd).

Measures 5–6 is a flawlessly executed three-note-per-string run up E natural minor. The shape moves a bit diagonally, as the first three sets of six notes require slight upward position shifts from 12th position to 14th position, and then to 16th position. The fourth set of six shifts just one fret up to 17th position. To perform these shifts more fluidly, do not anchor any fingers, but make it a practice to lift each as the next one comes down. The run peaks at D (♭7th) bending up to a high E (root).

Measure 7 descends with a blend of pentatonic leaps and chromaticism. After setting up the pace as that of 16ths, John throws us a curve at measure 8 by blasting into sextuplets and causing the four-note chromatic pattern to fall against the beat rhythmically.

At measure 9, we have a rising series of quintuplet patterns. Use straight alternate picking. This causes the first quintuplet to begin with a downstroke, the second with an upstroke, third with a down, the fourth up, and so on. This is rather unusual, but at least the pattern makes it clear that the first note on each strike is the "anchor" point relating to the underlying pulse. Build up speed slowly, and you will find that it is possible to feel runs in sets of five notes per beat. The run continues in measure 10 on the first string, now shifting these same five-note patterns into higher positions.

At measure 11, the pattern changes to four sets of seven notes. Again, while playing in sets of seven is unusual and at first will seem quite difficult (if not virtually impossible to get a handle on, rhythmically speaking), keep in mind that each set of seven notes is the very grouping played on each string. So to practice this, think of the *pattern* of the notes only. When you are finished with the pattern on that string, you switch to begin a similar pattern on the next string, feeling the "switch point" where you being the new string in each case as the downbeat (while playing to a metronome). At some point, when this all becomes second nature, you can attempt the run in time. John crams these notes in by feel and comes out "on his feet" on downbeat 2 to complete the run in 16ths.

Fig. 24

6:58

Guitar Solo

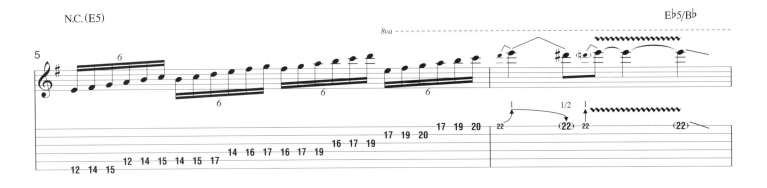

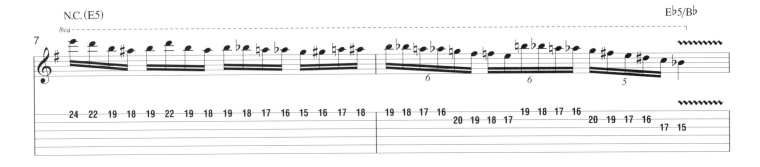

82

ENDLESS SACRIFICE

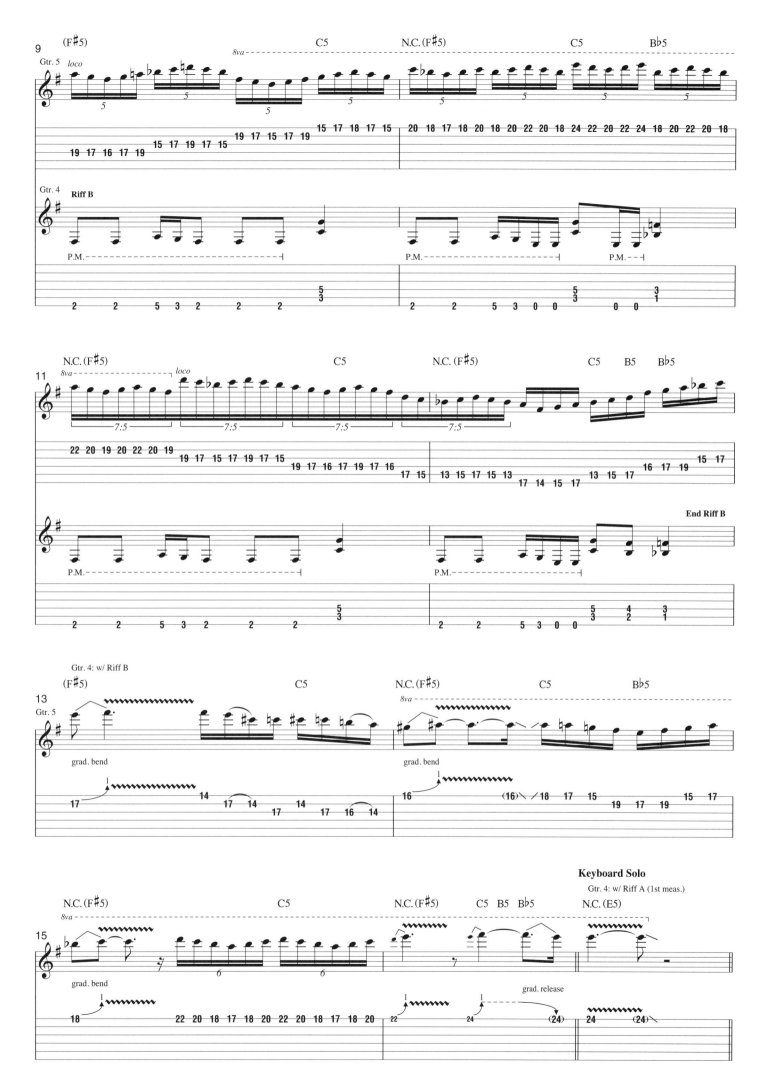

IN THE PRESENCE OF ENEMIES, PT. 1

(Systematic Chaos, 2007)
**Music by John Petrucci, Mike Portnoy, John Myung, Kevin LaBrie
and Jordan Rudess
Lyrics by John Petrucci**

Systematic Chaos is the ninth studio album by Dream Theater and, according to Portnoy, "a fitting description of the band in general." The first piece recorded was the 25-minute epic "In the Presence of Enemies," described by Petrucci as the "epitome of a Dream Theater creation." He describes it as "very progressive; very long." As it was felt that this piece was both a good opening for the album, as well as a closing, it was decided to split it into two parts.

Figure 25—Intro, Guitar Solo

The song opens into a distinct textural instrumentation that seems to recall Rush's "Freewill" (not shown). A repeating ostinato guitar riff with phaser is the "glue" holding the band together, while the other instruments play a variety of fill accents. At 0:30, things start rolling with a rather standard progression, but in trademark Dream Theater fashion, the band give it an entirely unpredictable feel due to use of the odd time signatures. At 1:42, the intro progresses into a series of accents with breaks while guitars blaze away in a repeating cycle of 32nd notes. It is easier to tap a double time pulse to this and feel the rhythm in 16ths. The pattern then becomes much easier to assimilate.

Measure 1 implies an A tonal center, with diminished backing chord accents. The notes G–A–B♭ (♭7–1–♭2) suggest the composite chord A half diminished flat 9. At measure 2, John takes us up a 4th to D, and then up another minor 3rd.

Measure 5 races down a composite diminished scale (part whole-half diminished and part half-whole diminished), outlining F#°7 and resolving to the G at the start of measure 6. Through measures 6–8, John transforms this to a G°7 using the same scale pattern as before. As this diminished scale rises, we label it C#°7 since we find it ultimately winds around to resolve to Dm. It does this, however, in two stages. You can feel the resolution happen at the start of measure 9 on the A note. You may be tempted to think this is therefore the harmonic target. But in fact, measures 9–12 form a single-note descending line that outlines Dm; A feels like a resolution because it is the 5th, a strong chord tone of D. The line tumbles down until finally coming to rest on the D chord in the accompaniment at measure 13 for the beginning of the guitar solo.

To contrast the thoroughly unpredictable nature of all the odd time signatures (dropping 16ths, eighths, and quarters seemingly randomly), we come to find relative ease and rest at the guitar solo with straight 4/4 time. The progression is Dm–C–G/B–B♭–D/A, drawn from D natural minor and Dorian (once again playing with the minor/major 6th as we've seen several times before).

John opts for a mellow, melodic approach, opening on A (5th). A half step bend at the end of measure 13 pulls from D Dorian, releasing back to B (6th) as a pickup motif into measure 14, which sits on G. Now over the C chord, G is the 5th chord tone, which gives us a very easy, purposeful sound. At measure 15, the chord motion gives us a form of B♭ chord, and the melody follows suit with F (5th), then walks down scalarly to tie up the phrase on the root, D. This phrase repeats at measure 17 with an added blues fill lick at the end of measure 20.

Measure 21 moves the progression to A (V), and the lead rises into a more soaring feeling. Added vibrato bar effects help make it smooth and seamless. On the repetition of the phrase starting at measure 25, we see a bit more decoration, culminating at measure 28 with a descending arpeggiated fill, followed by a quick ascending Am sweep.

Measures 29–36 move to Em and build slightly, with a quarter-note walking line resolving each four-measure phrase; the first one goes to Am and then we end up at Bb on the repeat. The energy is noticeably enhanced at measure 37. In measure 38, the E7 tension is clear. Yet, at measure 39–40 we still hear John pulling us back to the opening scalar "step down" motif to end the phrase—very compositionally minded. He continues to milk it out right to the end, adding a very tasteful set of decorations at measures 43–44.

Fig. 25

Full Band

Slow Demo
Gtr. 1 meas. 1–12

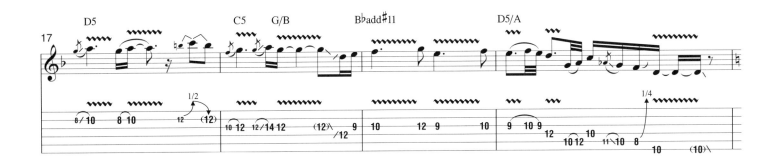

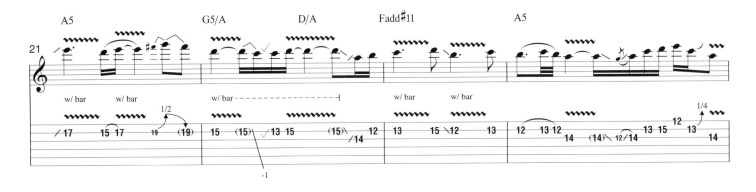

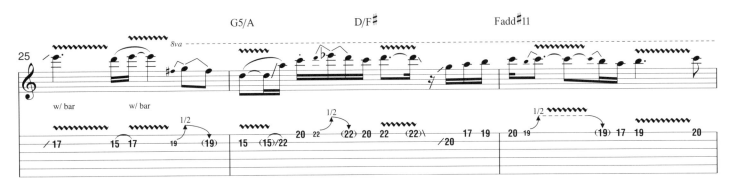

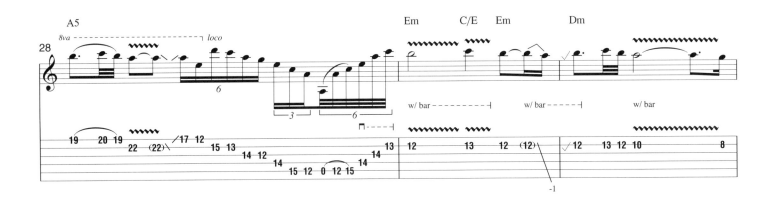

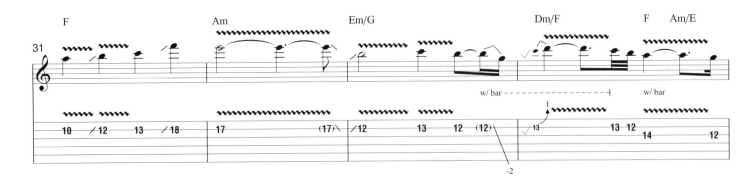

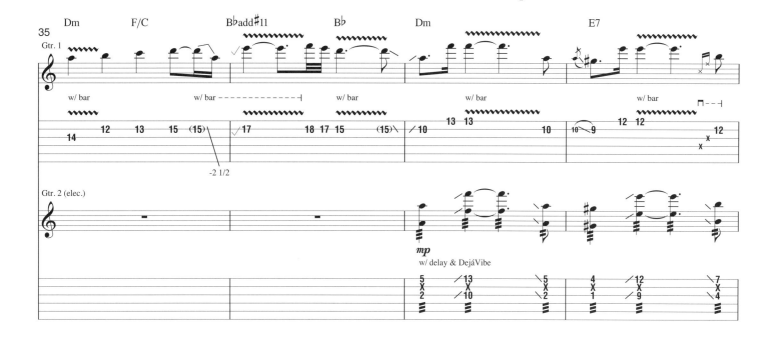

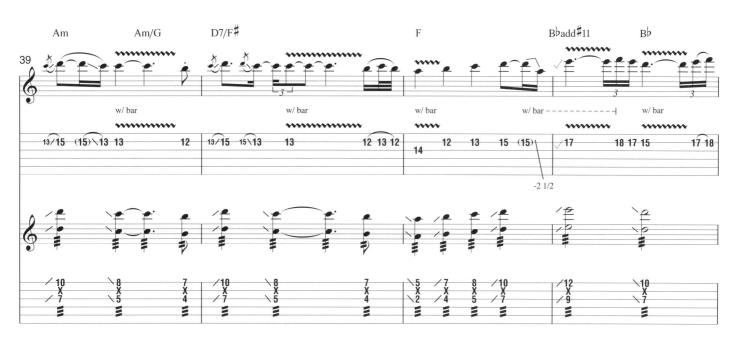

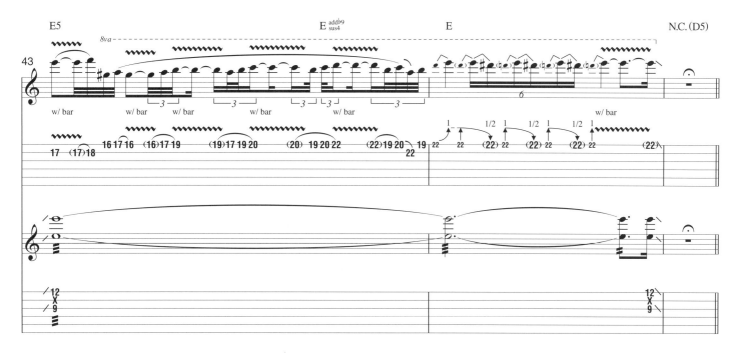

Figure 26—Bridge, Outro

The bridge groove is in 6/8 time—a compound meter—which means that it is counted in threes, "**1**–2–3–**4**–5–6." This means there are two compound beats per measure, each subdivided into a triplet. With an eighth equal to 181 bpm, the slower compound beats are therefore roughly 60 bpm. Now consider the syncopation. The first chord of the motif is the tritone dyad B/F (5–♭2) solidly on beat 1. This falls to E5 on the upbeat of 2. A low E-string palm mute acts as a pickup on upbeat 3, into the next motif, which reverses the dyad pattern. Getting the feel for this rhythm with its two syncopations in 6/8 time can be tricky at speed. If this is difficult for you, first try playing it without the low E until you get a feel for the rhythm of the two sustained dyads alone. Then add in the low palm mute.

The first dyads B/F–E5 imply an Em chord with added ♭2 (♭9), indicative of the Phrygian mode. Measures 3–4 raise the tritone ♭5 to a perfect 5th, creating standard power chords F5–E5 (♭2–1). Measures 5–6 involve a move to the bass note, D, but maintain the same F to E motion. This gives us the interval of a minor 10th (a minor 3rd an octave removed) and a 9th (a 2nd an octave removed) with F/D and E/D. The texture seems to spread apart more colorfully here with a move away from power chords. At measures 7–8, the bass note rises to B♭ under the same motion of F–E. This evokes the B♭ Lydian mode, characteristic of ♭VI and suggestive of the key center of D minor.

The eight-measure phrase repeats for measures 9–16. However, in true Dream Theater fashion, this time a few subdivisions of the beat have been omitted, just to throw you off a bit should you have become complacent in your listening. Here, the count becomes "**1** 2 3 **4** 5 6, **1** 2 3 **4** 5, **1** 2 3…" A pull-off helps differentiate this rhythmic change.

A short four-measure section caps off the bridge with a new vocal phrasing. The guitar line also shifts to mark this motif a bit differently with the inclusion of G♯ (major 3rd) in the bass under E. This helps set up a V–i cadence into A minor for the outro solo key.

At the guitar solo, in 6/8 time, we have four 32nd notes per eighth-note beat. So each compound beat actually has twelve 32nd notes. The best way to approach this is to feel all the subdivision beats—all six eighth-note beats per measure—and play each with four notes. So it's like 16ths in 4/4 time (at roughly 180 bpm) with the exception that here the 6/8 meter arranges the beats into sets of six. Therefore, string measure 21 together as six sets of four-note groupings. The sequence within the A natural minor shape will then become more apparent. Measure 22 begins with the same basic idea but contours the scale differently to send us into string 3 and 4 territory before coming back up.

At measure 23, John shifts the A minor diatonic scale to start at F (♭6th), reflecting the chord change to F5 (♭VI). Notice, however, that the basic contour in measures 23–24 remains similar to that of measures 21–22. He is building continuity here by presenting essentially the same idea but shifted in pitch to reinforce the chord tones of the underlying progression. At measures 25–26 this continues, raising the motif another scale step over Dm (more or less).

At measures 27–28, this occurs again over E, but this time the scale is altered into E Phrygian dominant (E–F–G♯–A–B–C–D) by sharping G. What would normally be E's minor 3rd thereby is transformed into a major 3rd, resulting in that characteristic brightness flanked by half steps (that differentiating "harmonic" quality popularized in the harmonic minor scale). Measures 29–30 shift it up a minor 3rd interval and repeat the motif, again over E and using the same E Phrygian dominant scale.

The section culminates in measures 31–32 over a chordal motion to B♭ (♭V), the tritone relative to E. John alters the scale to include B♭ and nails the important chord tones of B♭ in the descending run over each downbeat pulse. Consider each set of four notes (those grouped over each subdivision beat) as being a "decorated" version of the note that leads on that downbeat, and you will see beats 1–2–3 are B♭–F–B♭ (root–5th–root), and beats 4–5–6 are simply repeated verbatim, down an octave.

He strikes D (B♭'s major 3rd) as the low "directional shift" point and climbs through measure 32, again staying true to the scale altered to fit over B♭ and concluding at a high F♯ (B's 5th). This is a great example of John's purposeful and carefully composed approach to soloing, utilizing prominent chord tones to reinforce the harmonic aspects of lead lines even within high-speed, alternate picking runs.

Full Band

Slow Demo
Gtr. 3   meas. 21–33

Fig. 26

7:32

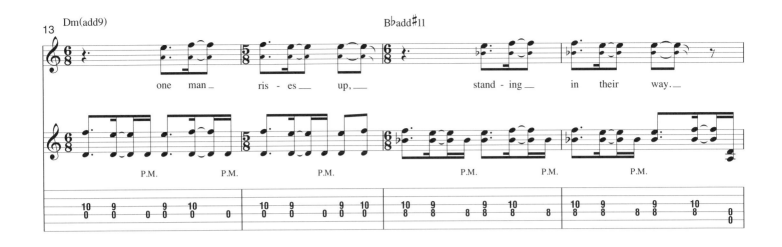

one man — ris - es — up, — stand - ing — in their way.

Re - demp - tion, ___ re - demp - tion — for — hu -

Outro

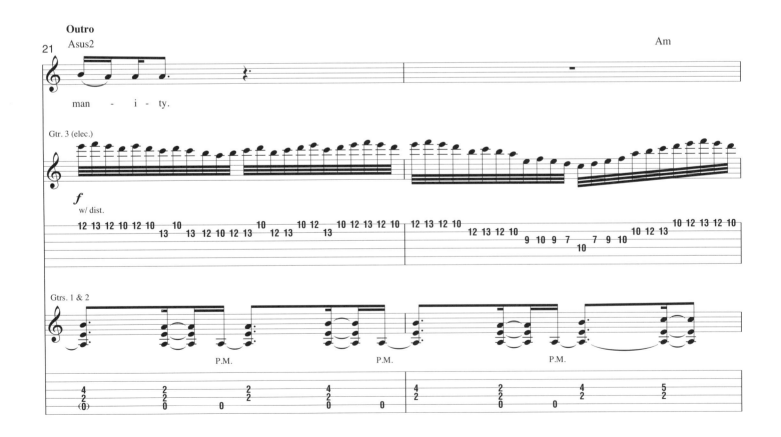

man - i - ty.

Gtr. 3 (elec.)

f
w/ dist.

Gtrs. 1 & 2

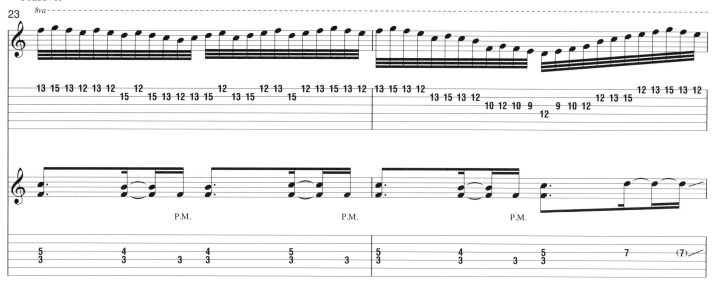

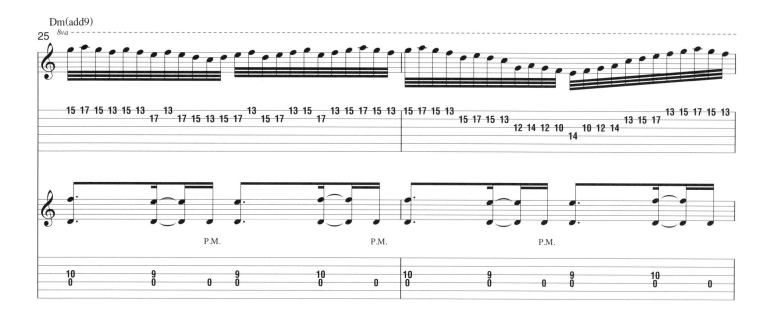

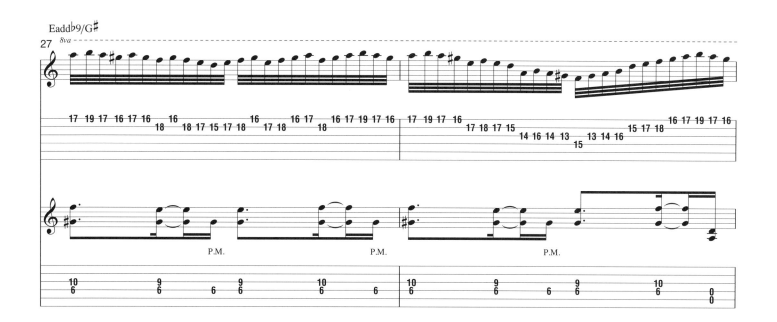

E5add♭9

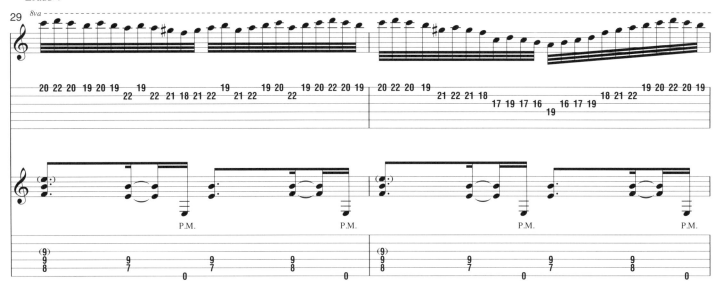

B♭5add♯11   Bm

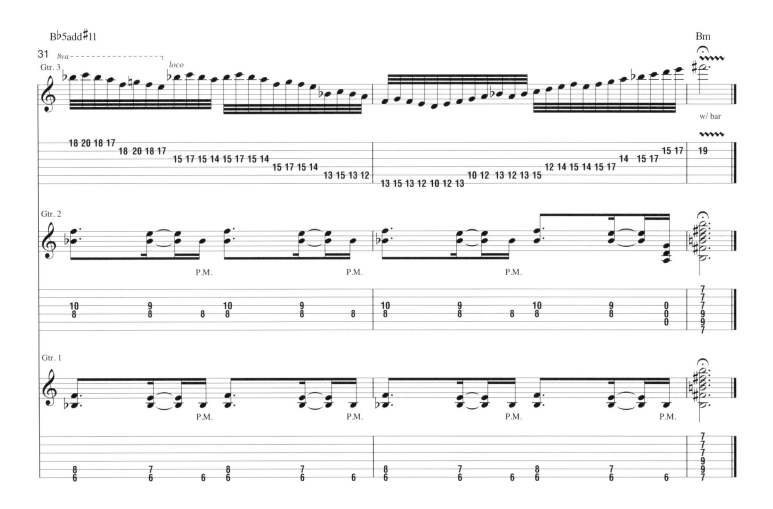

THE COUNT OF TUSCANY

(*Black Clouds & Silver Linings*, 2009)
Music by John Petrucci, Mike Portnoy, John Myung and Jordan Rudess
Lyrics by John Petrucci

Black Clouds & Silver Linings was released in 2009 and was the last studio album to feature drummer Mike Portnoy before his departure from the band in 2010. It debuted at number 6 on the *Billboard 200*—the first album to reach the Top 10 and marking Dream Theater's highest single week of album sales. "The Count of Tuscany" was written by John Petrucci and emerged after a personal encounter that he and his guitar tech had with the owner of a winery while on tour in Florence, Italy. John remarked in interviews that the old castle and its owner were both "very bizarre," inspiring him to pen the lyrics of the story.

Figure 27—Guitar Solo

The guitar solo at the intro of the song opens with a slow, singing melody over a G#m–B–F#–E progression, which is i–♭III–♭VII–♭VI in the key of G# minor. The focal pitches of the line are G# (root) over G#m, B–F# (root–5th) over B, C# (5th) over F#, and B (5th) over E.

At the conclusion of the phrase in measure 8, John rises up to a middle register E, followed by a six-note diatonic run as a pickup into a higher G# (root), beginning a second pass through the phrase. This time, however, John takes a completely different tack in the melody line. At measure 11, we have a classically inspired descending scale set against the repeated F# at fret 11. Additionally, the progression under this is altered, placing a first-inversion F# major chord (♭VII) here on its way up to B major (♭III) at measure 12. The lead guitar at measure 12 descends down the diatonic G# minor (B major) scale and is embellished with a quick trill and harmonized in 3rds by Gtr. 4, evoking even more of a melodic, classical feel.

At measure 13, we have a strong secondary melodic motif in the long pitches E–D#–B (1–7–5). Another pickup run up the G# minor scale at the end of measure 14 drops us into a repetition of that melodic motif, followed by an extension of it through the notes F#–G# (2–3 relative to the underlying E chord).

Fig. 27

*Gtr. 1 (acous.) doubled throughout;
 Gtr. 2 (elec.) w/ clean tone & chorus, doubled throughout

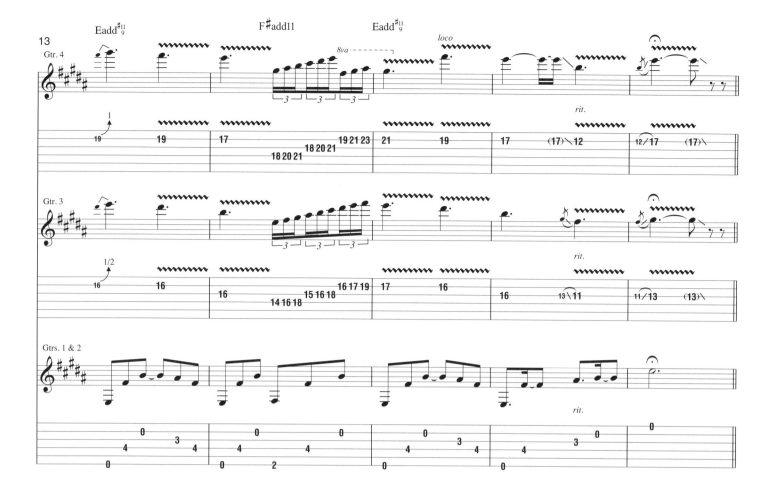

Figure 28—Interlude

The interlude at 3:02 is a brilliant synthesis of classical, progressive, and metal all rolled into one. Played in unison with the keys, the arpeggiated line first sets up a duple feel in 6/8—that is, with triplet 16ths on the compound downbeat and upbeat, the midpoint of each 6/8 compound beat is clearly communicated as a pulse. It sounds like 4/4 time with a triplet on each beat (usually written as 12/8). But in measure 2, suddenly the contour of the notes is shifted so that the accented upper voice seems to play in triplets relative to the previously identified pulse.

In measure 1, we have the leading notes of B–C#–D–C# (3–#4–5–#4), creating a Lydian sound over the G harmony. In measure 2, John opts to keep the pitches very nearly the same, as if to fully focus our attention on the changing element of rhythmic interest here, described above. The leading notes are the same B–C#–D (3–#4–5), until the chord change to A, with descending mirror notes E–D–C# (5–4–3 relative to A).

At measure 4, we get a surprise re-ordering of the notes, creating an added level of rhythmic interest. Then the whole phrase is reiterated up a minor 3rd at Bb major. John throws some more interesting curves at us in measure 8 with yet another contour shape.

Measures 9–10 complete the section, capping it off with a diminished, descending line identifying triplets. At measure 10, notice that the triplet feel continues, with the first 12 16th notes felt as four triplets. Then we see four extra 16ths added. So twelve 16ths (6/8 = 12/16) plus four extra 16ths, gives us a measure of 16/16—but felt as four triplets plus four 16ths. The final four 16ths become the "quarter pulse" of the 9/4 measure that follows. Alternatively, this could have been written as a 6/8 measure followed by a 1/4 measure and then a 9/4 measure of "breaks," which effectively functions as a means to stop time dramatically.

Fig. 28

Full Band

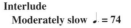

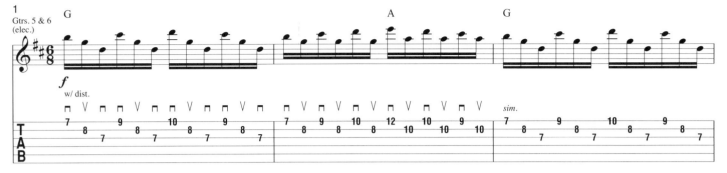

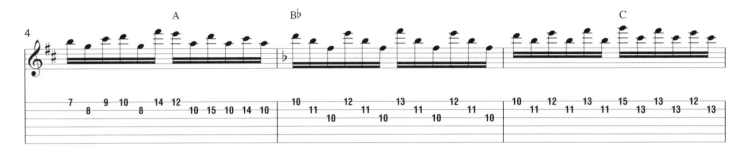

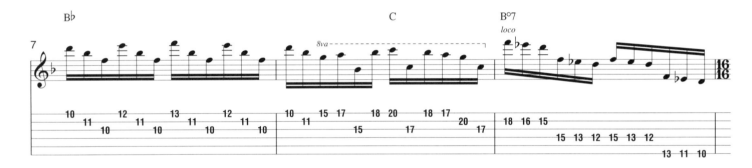

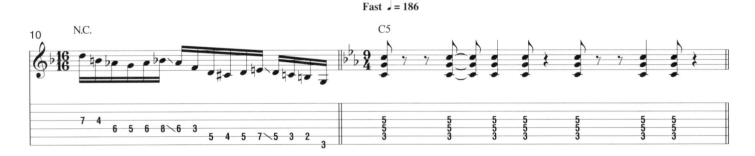

Figure 29—Intro to Verse

The band kicks into overdrive at 3:55, laying out the riff that will function to keep the momentum rolling under the verse that comes next (not shown). The rhythm with E5 power-chord accents interspersed with palm-muted low E pedal-tone chunks and 16th gallops is straightforward metal if you just took the first four beats and looped it. But in characteristic fashion, we see some timing irregularities added that move it unquestionably into Dream Theater mode. First, the gallop is repeated in a way to displace it against the underlying pulse. But even that is not enough! An extra gallop rhythm is tossed in, making the phrase an odd *nine* beats long. And *now* it's the perfect, defining progressive metal moment!

The chords in the upper-voice accents move through the pattern E5, C/E (a minor 6th interval, indicative of a first-inversion C major chord), an E major 3rd dyad, and finally E(b5) and Esus4 dyads to close the phrase. At measure 11, the riffing drops into the lower register, drawing upon E minor blues tones with added 5ths to form power chords.

Fig. 29

Figure 30—Interlude

The instrumental interlude at 9:37 contains several Dream Theater trademarks. First, the note patterns are built on sets of seven 16th notes. The first motif is G–C–G–F–G–F–E♭ (5–1–5–4–5–4–♭3) drawn from Cm. The next seven 16ths act as a "response" phrase to the first, drawn from B major with the notes B–F#–C#–B–B–B–A# (1–5–9–1–8–1–7). Measure 2 is then parallel to measure 1. First we see the Cm motif moved up a minor 3rd interval to become E♭m. D/F# "answers" this with a contour similar to before, except here an extra 16th note is added, giving us the full eight 16ths.

Measure 4 is identical to measure 2, except this time the extended D/F# "answer" phrase is extended even more to include a ninth 16th note. So the pattern within measures 1–4 is 7, 7, 7, 8, then 7, 7, 7, 9. This is repeated, using the second ending shown in measure 5. Here, even more notes are appended—three more to be precise—bringing the total number of 16ths in the D/F# answer motif to 12.

The third ending is the same as the first. Then the final ending extends even more, dropping to half speed for the final two.

Full Band

Slow Demo
Gtrs. 5 & 6   meas. 1–4

Fig. 30

9:37

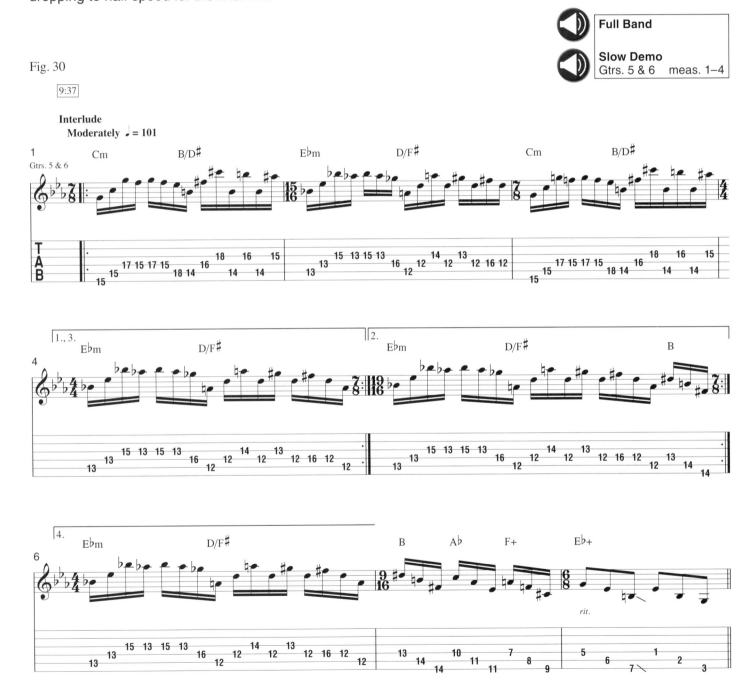

ON THE BACKS OF ANGELS

(*A Dramatic Turn of Events*, 2011)
Music by John Petrucci, John Myung and Jordan Rudess
Lyrics by John Petrucci

In September, 2010, Mike Portnoy announced he was leaving Dream Theater, citing burnout and the need for a break, as well as better relationships in other projects. According to John Petrucci, initially Mike did not want to leave the band—only to take a five-year break. He eventually dropped his request to one year. However, when the rest of the band rejected this proposal, he felt he had to quit. Mike was replaced with Berklee professor Mike Mangini.

A Dramatic Turn of Events followed in 2011, opening at number 8 on the *Billboard 200*, and the song "On the Backs of Angels," the album's lead track and first single, was nominated for a Grammy in 2012.

Figure 31—Intro, Verse

After a long intro build, the band drives hard on an E5–G5, and E5–C#(♭5)–Bb5 power chord riff starting at 1:55. Interestingly, this riff is in straight 4/4 time—unusual for Dream Theater, and allowing for a somewhat more accessible feel in terms of the broader audience. Nevertheless, John incorporates some surprise rhythmic twists, such as the prominent accent on beat 4 (with G5 and C#(♭5)). This, when combined with a drum part that seems to further obscure the standard rock backbeat of "snare on 2 and 4," gives the phrase a quite progressive sound, even as the pulse is easily followed. At measure 9, the guitar breaks down to a set of E5 accent jabs in a repeating 5/4 measure. In measure 11, Petrucci walks down into the verse using E natural minor.

The verse molds together two previous motifs: the accent E5 idea from measure 9 and the ending of the intro riff at measure 4 (beats 2–4).

Full Band

Slow Demo
Gtrs. 1 & 2 meas. 1–8

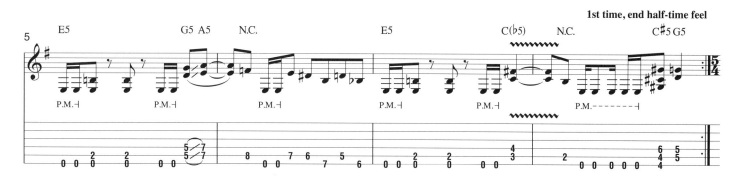

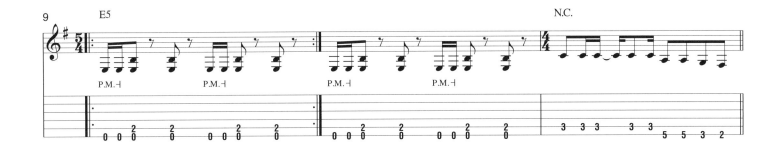

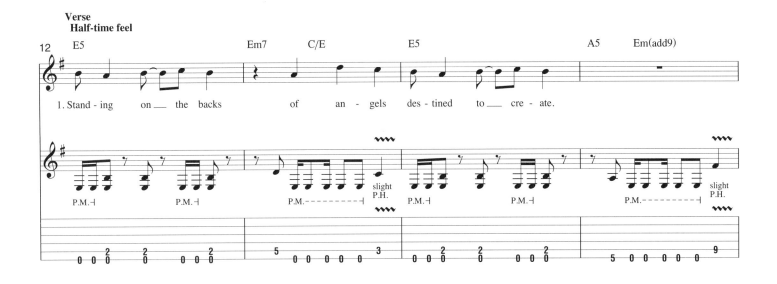

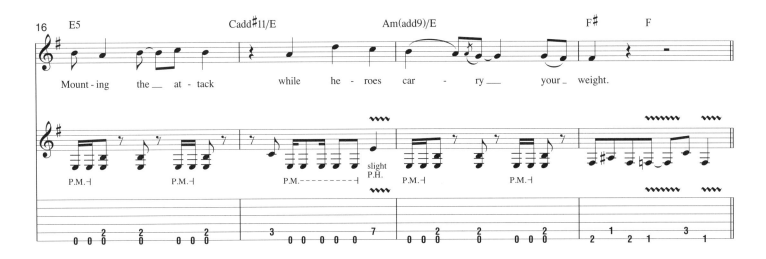

Figure 32—Pre-Chorus, Interlude, Chorus

The pre-chorus at 3:28 opens up to roll on palm-muted 16ths on the low E string. The motif intersperses upper-voiced tones on the first two 16ths of beats 1, 3, and 4 of each measure. Notice how measures 3 and 4 are basically a mirror of 1 and 2, except the pitches of the upper-voiced tones progress downward. Measures 5–8 bring the low E pedal up an octave into the same register as the moving upper voices, but the pitches stay true to outline the same harmonic territory.

The interlude is a short but majestic and melodic solo. John climbs through chord tones of the underlying progression Em–D–G–C–Bm (i–♭VII–♭III–♭VI–v). This would be fairly standard rock territory except for the unexpected timing, causing the chord changes to feel a bit haphazard and lending a bit more rhythmic interest. A unison single-note line in measures 14–15 drops us via sequenced descent down to E (V) in preparation for the Am chorus to follow at measure 17.

ON THE BACKS OF ANGELS

The chorus is lent a completely different texture as John allows the strings to ring together prominently. He moves through the upper tones of Am, B–A–B–C–B–A (2–1–2–♭3–2–1), while still firmly attached to A5 (1–5) underneath. At measures 19–20, as the progression moves to F (♭VI), John focuses on the common tone A, leaving it in the bass and repeating the same B–A–B–C–B–A motif in the upper voice (now #4–3–#4–5–#4–3 relative to F).

Next, in a very non-standard and non-formulaic move, we see the following four-measure phrase, which literally has very little in common with the first part of the chorus. (Generally choruses repeat the progression and melody motif here.) Instead, we see the chorus guitar motif from measure 17, excerpted and shortened, presented as four quarter notes in measure 21. The bass note is walked down incrementally as A–G–F#–F (1–♭7–6–♭6) and then B♭ (♭2) is presented, leaning hard to resolve to the Am that follows, beginning the chorus passage over again at measure 25.

Just when you thought it would be safe to assume that we are back in familiar territory, and expecting perhaps to repeat the chorus, that comfort is withdrawn. Instead, measures 27–28 are *not* a repetition of 19–20. The chord progression here replaces F with Dm (the relative minor). Measures 29–32, however, are a bit more regular, as they are an exact duplication of measures 21–24.

Fig. 32

3:28

Full Band

Chorus

Figure 33—Guitar Solo

This is perhaps one of John Petrucci's finest soloing moments, waxing both melodic and purposeful—even graceful—while building with both tension and precision. And although he pushes to the point of fast sextuplets at the climax, it is far from unapproachable.

The key is E minor. John opens with a pickup B (5th) to F# (2nd) and draws out its unresolved quality hard until sliding up to B (5th) via G (♭3rd). Against lower octave Bs, he descends the E minor scale using B–A–G (5–4–♭3). The last beat of measure 2 is a four-note approach to the target pitch F# (2nd), the next scale tone in line from the preceding descent.

In measure 3, John gives us a powerful melodic tension with the A# (#4th relative to the key center) and further pushes its importance by laying it in place to rhythmically mirror the first resolution in measure 1 (to B). So in a sense, where measure 1 resolved, measure 3 repeats the phrasing motif and at that point moves to a strong melodic tension. Yet the harmonic case for this pitch is solid; it is the major 3rd above F# (the important target note in this measure), and as such, A# is in fact a harmony to F# (as well as the root of the underlying harmony of A#°7). John builds the harmony further, as he rises next to C# (the 5th above our F# target note), spelling out the full F# major triad.

At measures 5–6, we come to Am for two measures, as John rises through Am triad arpeggios and A minor pentatonic shapes (using his trademark practice of stretching out over two boxes simultaneously and thereby allowing repeated tones played on different strings to make the lick somewhat less predictable).

At measure 7, we would expect the progression—which has been following a two-measure-per-chord pattern (Em–A#°–Am)—to resolve back to Em for the final two measures. And we would be amiss. John has the backing chord extend Am over measure 7, where he plays with the same 2nd-to-chord-tone resolution with which he opened the solo. Only after this surprise Am extension does the backing chord shift to Em to complete the eight-measure progression. To help mark this Em in measure 8 as the end of the progression, and to differentiate it from the Em that follows in measure 9, the rhythm guitar plays it with the moving bass line G–F# (♭3–2), which then drops convincingly to the E (root) at the start of measure 9, starting the progression over again.

But of course that would also be too simple—why play something twice the same way when you can change it? The repeat of the progression replaces A#°7/E with A#°7/C#, and C replaces Am in measures 13–14.

Over this, the lead in measure 9 applies the same focus on F# (2nd) as in measure 1, except this time it has been applied in eighths amidst a pedal tone, and an octave higher than previously. At measure 10, we again see the motif of B–A–G (5–4–♭3) coming down the E minor scale to hit the targeted F# (2nd) at the start of measure 11. A beautiful arpeggio flourish enters in measure 13. Based in C major, notice the added color tone A (6th) in beat 2. At measure 14, John raises it into what may appear at first to be an Em shape. But over the backing C chord, and given the fact that in beat 2 we have the lower portion of a C major triad, in fact this is correctly viewed as an extended C major 7th chord: C–E–G–B–E–G–B (1–3–5–7–3–5–7).

The diatonic alternate picking run marks the conclusion of the solo in common Petrucci fashion. The first two sextuplets establish the descending contour, and the next two simply repeat it an octave lower, continuing the descent. At measure 16, a third repetition begins but turns around midway to begin the final ascent.

Fig. 33

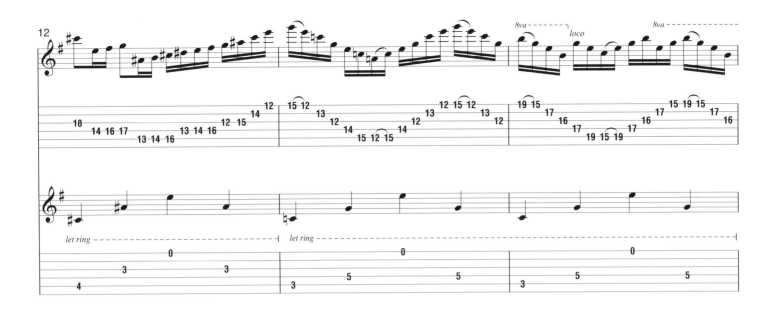

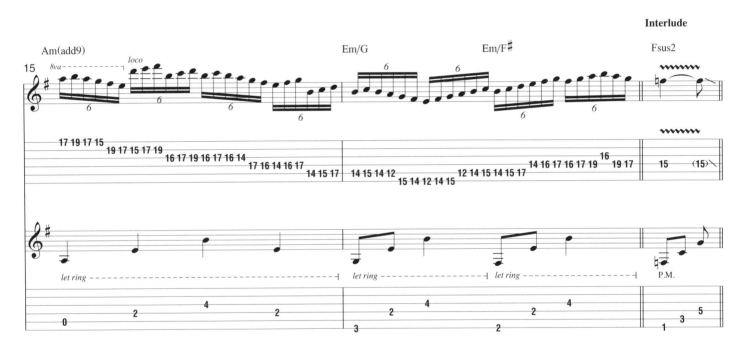

BREAKING ALL ILLUSIONS

(*A Dramatic Turn of Events*, 2011)
Music by John Petrucci, John Myung and Jordan Rudess
Lyrics by John Petrucci and John Myung

Figure 34—Guitar Solo

"Breaking All Illusions" is track 8 on *A Dramatic Turn of Events*. Although the song delivers many "Petrucci-isms," he also gives us a very distinctive and unusual treat at 7:11 with an iconically bluesy and masterful solo, effectively showcasing his wide versatility as a guitarist. This is no metal guitarist rendition of the blues; he goes deep into the style before eventually pulling it around into his own trademarked territory. Let's take a look…

To get a more laid-back, bluesy tone, roll the volume knob down to reduce the gain level. The key is D minor, and the progression is Gm–Dm (iv–i), with each chord lasting four measures. Phrase 1 opens with the initial motif over Gm. The target notes are B♭ (♭3rd) on beat 3 of measure 1, A (2nd) on beat 1 of measure 2, and G (root) on beat 3 of measure 2. Pickup notes decorate and step into each target note. In measures 5–8, the motif repeats now on Dm, utilizing A–G–F (5–4–♭3). This time, John pulls time quite freely, dragging hard to lag behind the beat for added effect. Also, a prominent rake articulation decorates the opening of the second phrase, and he further embellishes the end of the line, dressing up the fall to the final D (root) with a quick hammer/pull/slide, followed by a bluesy hammer with the third finger and immediate slide to the same note with the first finger—an authentic blues technique that doubles the note and places extra attention on the slide articulation.

At measure 9, a tasteful triplet climb edges up first using non-chord tones and then joins solid harmonic ground at B♭ (♭3rd). The first four notes of the climb, A–C–E–F (2–4–6–♭7), are in fact all the extended jazz tones within the diatonic key: ♭7–9–11–13. Therefore, it's no surprise they offer such a colorful presentation. At the end of measure 9, John goes diatonic up through Gm. Measure 10 descends using 6ths. B♭–D (♭3–5) identifies Gm as a 6th dyad; A–C (2–4) are the next scale tones in the descent on their way to G–B♭ (1–♭3), although John omits the final low B♭ of the pattern and simply hangs on the root, G. Again, notice that he drags time here in a big way to draw out and magnify the full bluesy quality. The phrase closes over Dm, first with a pre-bend to F (♭3rd), recalling the previous hammer/slide blues motif seen in measures 7–8, and then he gets more aggressive with a low-register D minor pentatonic lick in triplets. This completes the first 16-measure section.

The energy picks up markedly at measure 17 with a rhythmically displaced lick that, at first look, appears to be D minor pentatonic box 1. Roll up the volume knob a bit at this point. The note pattern is quite stock, but in fact this is played over Gm. So it is really G minor pentatonic box 4 and relies heavily on A (2nd), in place of and omitting B♭ (♭3rd). In addition, look beyond the note pattern here and pay careful attention to the rhythmic aspect of the lick; this is where all the feel and nuance lie. The completion of the Gm phrase (measures 18–20) leaves the blues territory, and we see John shift toward his common lead stylings with straight 16th alternate picking and sequenced contours, after which he breaks into a sextuplet run in G Dorian.

At measure 21, we are back to D minor, and John nails a high D and then descends in pentatonic/blues box 1, which sounds refreshingly familiar. He reaches up to A (5th) and bends it a wide minor 3rd up to C (♭7th) to breathe in some tonal variety after such a strong focus on the root, D.

Measure 28 features an interesting set of arpeggio sweeps. Over Gm, the most prominent pitch in each sweep is the last, and we see these rising straight across the strings at fret 17, as G–C–E–A (1–4–6–2). The sweeps themselves color it further outside of Gm chord tones, using a plethora of extended jazz harmony pitches. Then bluesy bending antics pull us strongly back to the blues roots over Dm at measure 29, and the phrase concludes in measures 30–32 via a strong descending blues line with classic hammer-pull embellishments in D minor pentatonic/blues box 1.

Roll up the volume knob fully at measure 33, as we leave the blues zone and things get majestic when the progression moves to B♭–Gm–C–A (♭VI–iv–♭VII–V), which acts to set up a strong harmonic move to return to the tonic, Dm (at measure 41). The phrase energy rises as the chords now pass by twice as fast (every two measures instead of every four). In the lead, John approaches these chords diatonically, weaving in chord tones of the underlying progression, creating a purposeful, melodic line that emphasizes the feel of the progression.

This flows beautifully into the distant, wistful melody beginning at measure 41. This is played over a new progression of Dm–C–B♭–Gm (i–♭VII–♭VI–iv), which nails the tonic hard. Again the energy rises by virtue of having the chords pass by twice as fast; they now pass every measure. After two repetitions of this, the progression changes again, and we cap off the solo with B♭–Am–G (♭VI–v–IV), then B♭–C–D5 (♭VI–♭VII–i).

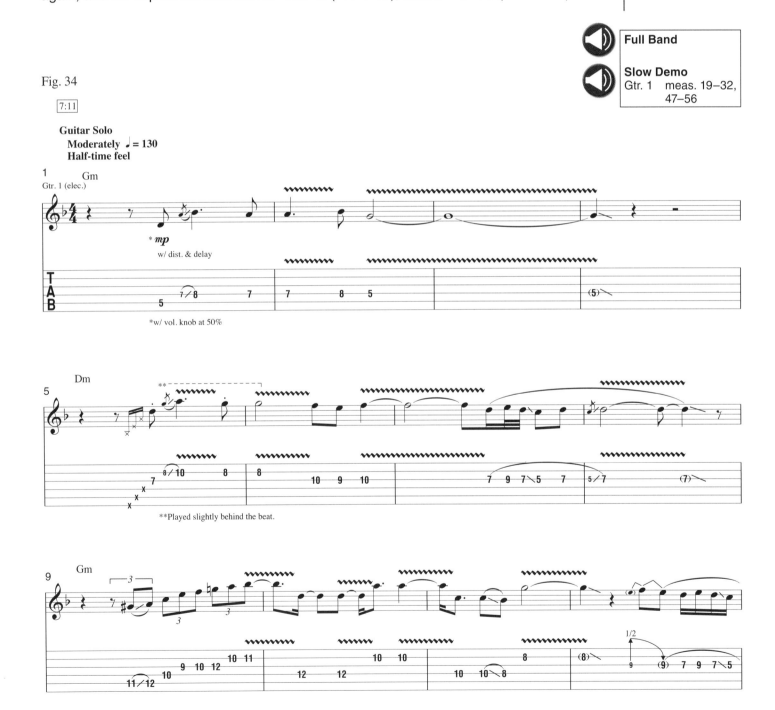

Full Band

Slow Demo
Gtr. 1   meas. 19–32, 47–56

Fig. 34

7:11

Guitar Solo
Moderately ♩ = 130
Half-time feel

*w/ dist. & delay

*w/ vol. knob at 50%

**Played slightly behind the beat.

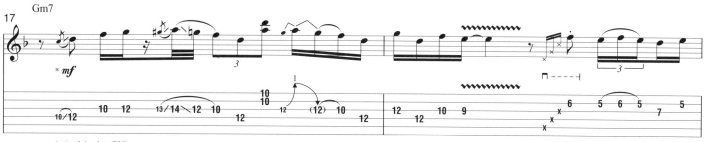

*w/ vol. knob at 75%

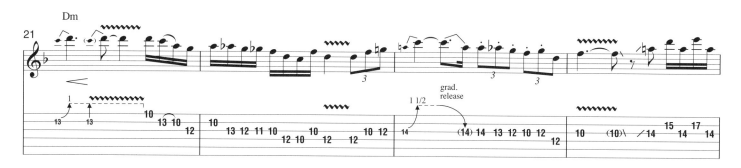

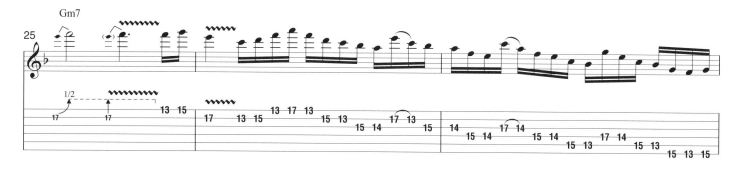

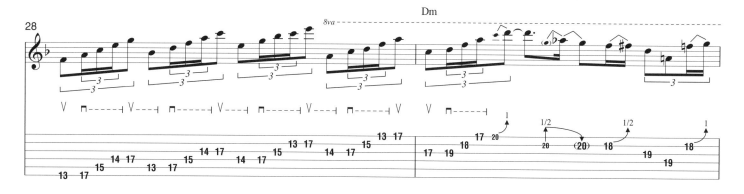

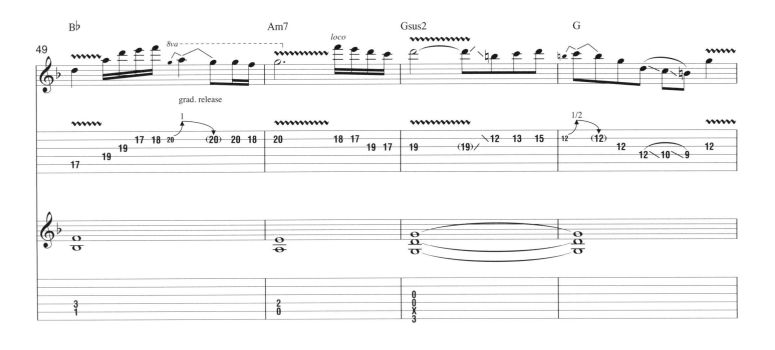

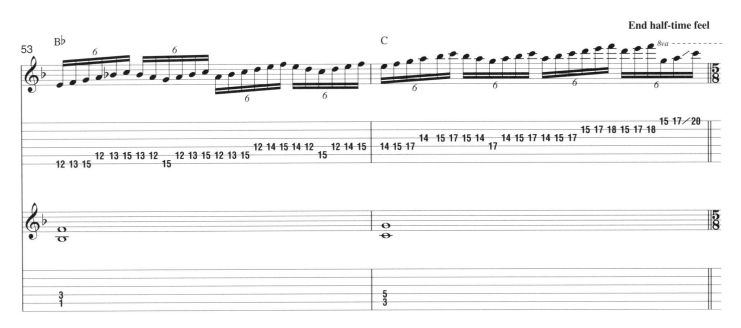

Interlude

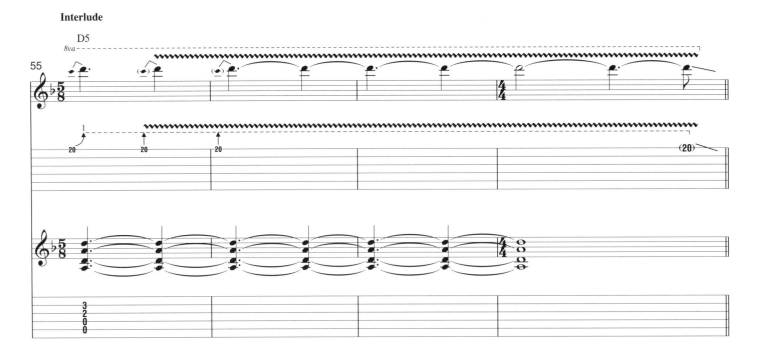

BEHIND THE VEIL

(*Dream Theater*, 2013)
Music by John Petrucci, Jordan Rudess, John Myung, James LaBrie and Mike Mangini
Lyrics by John Petrucci

The self-titled album *Dream Theater* is the band's twelfth studio effort and was released in 2013. "Behind the Veil," track 6, features a bit more of a simplified hard rock/ metal approach in many of its primary sections, such as the riff, verse, and chorus. Yet the progressive element is clearly there in the extended interludes, long intro, multiple but related riffs, and generally non-formulaic and unpredictable song structure.

Figure 35—Intro, Verse, Pre-Chorus, Chorus

The intro builds for over two minutes and then breaks down at 2:13 to a simple, hard rock riff in E minor. Although John uses a seven-string guitar in standard tuning here for Gtr. 1, you can fairly easily transform the riff to be played on a six-string. (The main motif in measures 1–3 doesn't use the seventh string at all. Then you can simply raise the low B note and D5–E5 portion at measures 3–4 up an octave.) In any case, be sure to perform the rests as clean and full stops, without fret muting noise, by using both hands to deaden the strings at precisely the correct times. Notice that the end of the phrase contains a 3/4 measure, dropping out the last beat of the phrase in characteristic Dream Theater style.

The guitar riff is demoted to a subordinate role, sliding under the vocal at the start of the verse by reducing the energy down to single notes. Also, palm mutes are added, giving the part a bit more of a rolling momentum, rather than the angular start/stop heard in the previous riff breakdown. The chord symbols reflect composite tonality, including both the riff, vocal, and chromatically descending keyboard line.

The pre-chorus takes the energy down a notch with an arpeggiated, clean texture. This is played on six-string guitar and doubled on acoustic. In 5/4 time, F♯ and open G are forced over Bm–C–Am (v–♭VI–iv) as a common-tone motif in beats 4–5 of each measure. Em completes the progression in measure 24 over a walking bass line. Measures 25–28 mirror this with an altered ending.

The chorus is unusual for Dream Theater: a big vocal hook over "loud and proud" hard rock power chords played in straight 4/4 time. The progression is E5–B5–C5 (i–v–♭VI), ending with a tag of C5–B5 accents followed by C5–D5 accents. It's a simple, standard, Aeolian mode progression in power chords. Gtr. 7, however, adds some texture in palm-muted eighths. Over Em, we have B (5th) as the pedal tone, and leading notes G–F♯–E–F♯ (♭3–2–1–2) draw from E natural minor. Over Bm, John plays an arpeggiated Bm triad, B–D–F♯ (1–♭3–5). Over C, we have the same as Em, except that the pedal moves up a half step to C, drawing out the quality of C Lydian with the notes C–G–F♯–E (1–5–♯4–3). At measure 32, he outlines G and D arpeggios.

Fig. 35

Full Band

2:13

Intro
Moderately fast ♩ = 152

*w/ Gtr. 2 on repeats

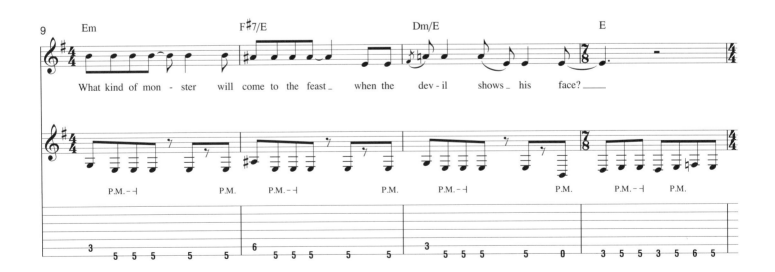

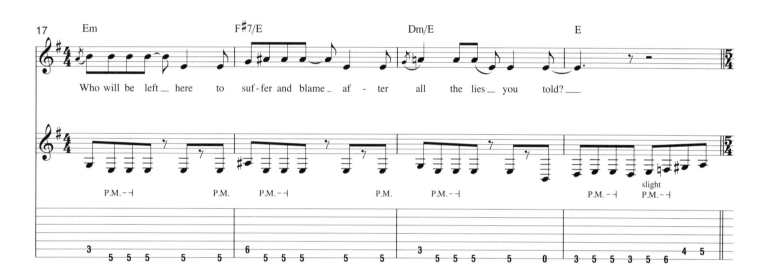

Pre-Chorus

Gtrs. 1 & 2 tacet

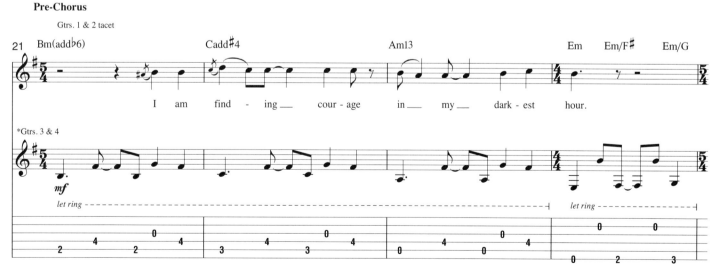

*Gtr. 3 (elec.) w/ clean tone & chorus, doubled throughout;
Gtr. 4 (acous.) doubled throughout

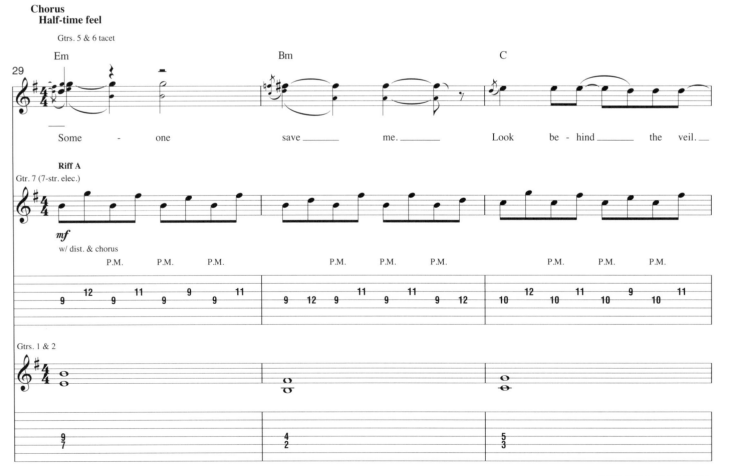

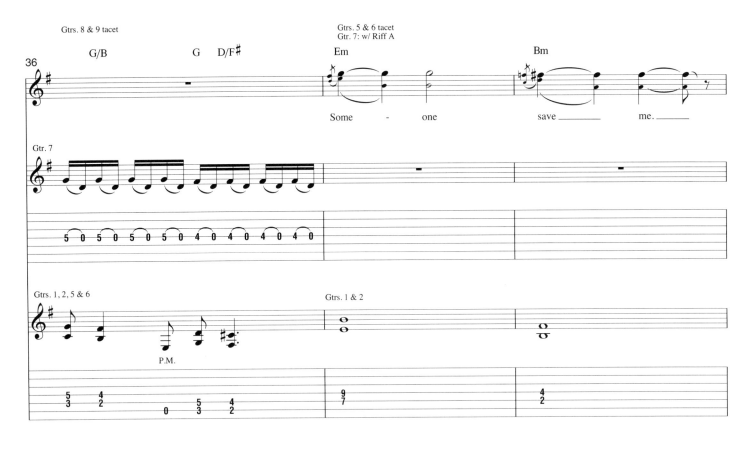

Figure 36—Interlude, Guitar Solo

The interlude at 4:45 is typical of Dream Theater: a single-note line in eighths written in 7/8 time to muck with the pulse. Revolving around a C in measures 1–4, the notes C–G–C–D–F#–E–D (1–5–1–2–#4–3–2) define the C Lydian mode. At measures 5–8, John shifts to Em with E–B–E–F#–A–G–F# (1–5–1–2–4–♭3–2). Then it's back to C for four measures, and then D. The whole interlude then, harmonically speaking, is C–Em–C–D. In the key of E minor, this is ♭VI–i–♭VI–♭VII.

Of particular significance at the beginning of the solo is the fact that the riff here identifies seven beats per measure, with two measures on each chord. It takes a little getting used to the feel of soloing over 14-beat phrases. The basic progression is Em–C–Em–C at measures 17–24. John favors the chord tones over each respective chord: E–G–B over Em and C–E–G over C. Technically, while over Em, the scale runs are that of E natural minor, and while over C, the same notes become C Lydian. The easiest way to approach this is to see the E minor scale patterns throughout but highlight the Em arpeggios while over Em and the C major arpeggios when over the C.

The guitar solo enters slowly in the middle register on G (♭3rd) to F# (2nd), followed by a quick quintuplet run up E natural minor. The primary feature in measure 18 is arpeggio sweeping, starting with Em and then a prominent Asus4 near the end of the measure. We see John's penchant for double picking in a sequenced, arpeggiated line at measure 21—a technique that enables a higher energy due to alternate picking 16ths. And yet the fact that the pitches move at the speed of eighths makes it easier for the listener to follow each note.

The run at measure 24 is particularly difficult, as the sequence pattern is actually in fours but played as even quintuplets rhythmically. There is no easy way to master this; it is the result of years of quintuplet practice. Whereas the quintuplet runs we saw earlier were easier by virtue of the pattern on the guitar itself being arranged in sets of five notes, here the pattern of the sequence is actually in sets of fours. So you must be able to play the sets of four by habit to such a degree that you hardly have to think about them, while focusing your attention on the feel of playing that pattern in "fives." It requires a sort of "split awareness." But hopefully, by this point you will have mastered the "easier" quintuplets and gained a feel for these such that this more difficult approach is now within reach.

John ventures into Am territory at measure 25, now switching chords faster. At measure 26, we have an F#°7 arpeggio played with string skipping, followed by ascending diminished 7th sweeps á la Yngwie Malmsteen in measure 27. This culminates with a high-speed, two-handed tapping line at measure 28. Of particular notice is how John has intentionally mismatched the patterns with the timing; the patterns identify sets of four, but he plays this in sextuplets, causing a more interesting rhythmic interaction. This approach makes it a bit harder for the listener to grasp exactly what is happening, and therefore it sounds faster and more complex than it really is.

At measure 29, John opts to shift the feel into that of classical resolutions, racing through F#7, which resolves to B7 in measure 30 and E in measure 31. All the speed antics are over, and it's arena rock time for measures 31–36, amidst a pounding half-time drum pulse in straight 4/4 time. Then it's a balls-out, speed picking, pentatonic-based climax á la Scorpions or West Coast style late '80s hair metal.

Fig. 36

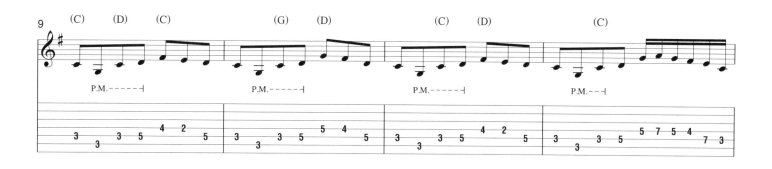

Guitar Solo

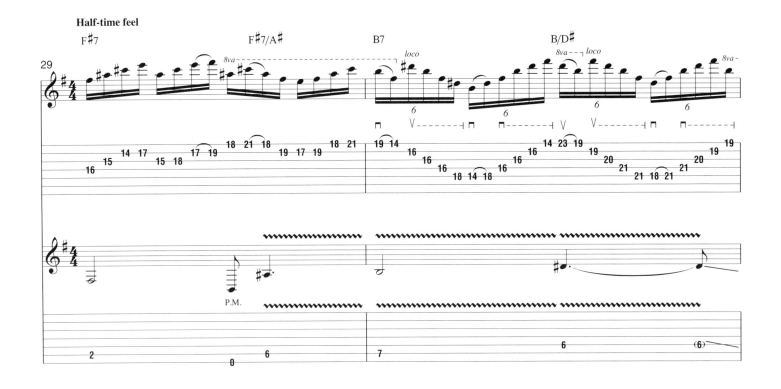

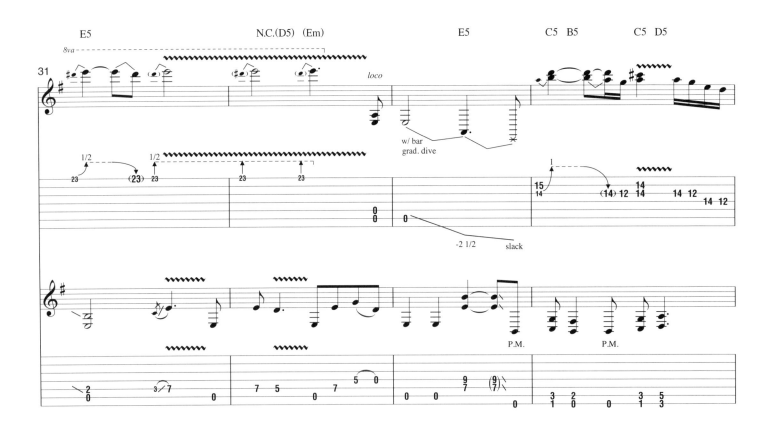

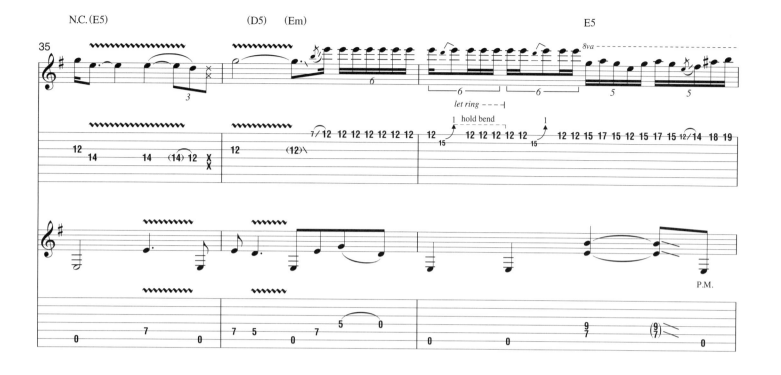

GUITAR NOTATION LEGEND

Guitar music can be notated three different ways: on a *musical staff*, in *tablature*, and in *rhythm slashes*.

RHYTHM SLASHES are written above the staff. Strum chords in the rhythm indicated. Use the chord diagrams found at the top of the first page of the transcription for the appropriate chord voicings. Round noteheads indicate single notes.

THE MUSICAL STAFF shows pitches and rhythms and is divided by bar lines into measures. Pitches are named after the first seven letters of the alphabet.

TABLATURE graphically represents the guitar fingerboard. Each horizontal line represents a string, and each number represents a fret.

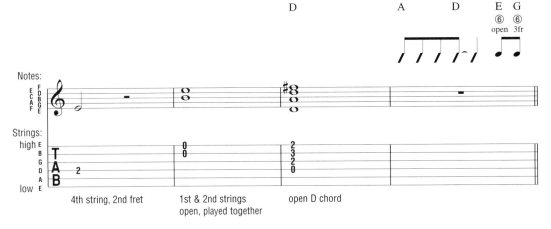

4th string, 2nd fret

1st & 2nd strings open, played together

open D chord

Definitions for Special Guitar Notation

HALF-STEP BEND: Strike the note and bend up 1/2 step.

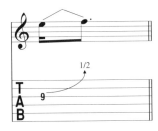

BEND AND RELEASE: Strike the note and bend up as indicated, then release back to the original note. Only the first note is struck.

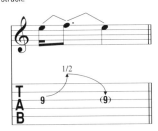

VIBRATO: The string is vibrated by rapidly bending and releasing the note with the fretting hand.

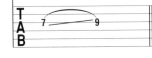

LEGATO SLIDE: Strike the first note and then slide the same fret-hand finger up or down to the second note. The second note is not struck.

WHOLE-STEP BEND: Strike the note and bend up one step.

PRE-BEND: Bend the note as indicated, then strike it.

WIDE VIBRATO: The pitch is varied to a greater degree by vibrating with the fretting hand.

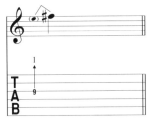

SHIFT SLIDE: Same as legato slide, except the second note is struck.

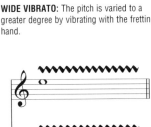

GRACE NOTE BEND: Strike the note and immediately bend up as indicated.

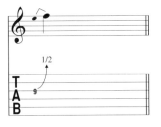

PRE-BEND AND RELEASE: Bend the note as indicated. Strike it and release the bend back to the original note.

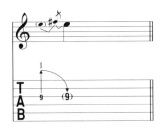

HAMMER-ON: Strike the first (lower) note with one finger, then sound the higher note (on the same string) with another finger by fretting it without picking.

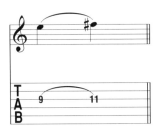

TRILL: Very rapidly alternate between the notes indicated by continuously hammering on and pulling off.

SLIGHT (MICROTONE) BEND: Strike the note and bend up 1/4 step.

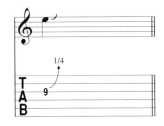

UNISON BEND: Strike the two notes simultaneously and bend the lower note up to the pitch of the higher.

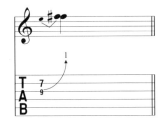

PULL-OFF: Place both fingers on the notes to be sounded. Strike the first note and without picking, pull the finger off to sound the second (lower) note.

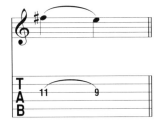

TAPPING: Hammer ("tap") the fret indicated with the pick-hand index or middle finger and pull off to the note fretted by the fret hand.

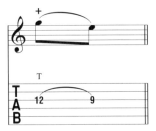

NATURAL HARMONIC: Strike the note while the fret-hand lightly touches the string directly over the fret indicated.

PINCH HARMONIC: The note is fretted normally and a harmonic is produced by adding the edge of the thumb or the tip of the index finger of the pick hand to the normal pick attack.

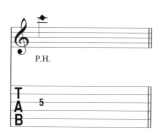

HARP HARMONIC: The note is fretted normally and a harmonic is produced by gently resting the pick hand's index finger directly above the indicated fret (in parentheses) while the pick hand's thumb or pick assists by plucking the appropriate string.

PICK SCRAPE: The edge of the pick is rubbed down (or up) the string, producing a scratchy sound.

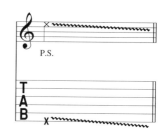

MUFFLED STRINGS: A percussive sound is produced by laying the fret hand across the string(s) without depressing, and striking them with the pick hand.

PALM MUTING: The note is partially muted by the pick hand lightly touching the string(s) just before the bridge.

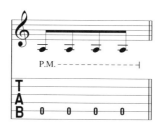

RAKE: Drag the pick across the strings indicated with a single motion.

TREMOLO PICKING: The note is picked as rapidly and continuously as possible.

ARPEGGIATE: Play the notes of the chord indicated by quickly rolling them from bottom to top.

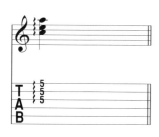

VIBRATO BAR DIVE AND RETURN: The pitch of the note or chord is dropped a specified number of steps (in rhythm), then returned to the original pitch.

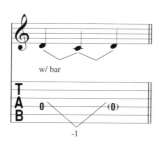

VIBRATO BAR SCOOP: Depress the bar just before striking the note, then quickly release the bar.

VIBRATO BAR DIP: Strike the note and then immediately drop a specified number of steps, then release back to the original pitch.

Additional Musical Definitions

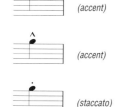

(accent) • Accentuate note (play it louder).

(accent) • Accentuate note with great intensity.

(staccato) • Play the note short.

• Downstroke

V • Upstroke

D.S. al Coda • Go back to the sign (%), then play until the measure marked "*To Coda*," then skip to the section labelled "**Coda**."

D.C. al Fine • Go back to the beginning of the song and play until the measure marked "*Fine*" (end).

Rhy. Fig. • Label used to recall a recurring accompaniment pattern (usually chordal).

Riff • Label used to recall composed, melodic lines (usually single notes) which recur.

Fill • Label used to identify a brief melodic figure which is to be inserted into the arrangement.

Rhy. Fill • A chordal version of a Fill.

tacet • Instrument is silent (drops out).

• Repeat measures between signs.

• When a repeated section has different endings, play the first ending only the first time and the second ending only the second time.

NOTE: Tablature numbers in parentheses mean:
1. The note is being sustained over a system (note in standard notation is tied), or
2. The note is sustained, but a new articulation (such as a hammer-on, pull-off, slide or vibrato) begins, or
3. The note is a barely audible "ghost" note (note in standard notation is also in parentheses).

HAL•LEONARD GUITAR PLAY•ALONG

This series will help you play your favorite songs quickly and easily. Just follow the tab and listen to the audio to the hear how the guitar should sound, and then play along using the separate backing tracks. Mac or PC users can also slow down the tempo without changing pitch by using the CD in their computer. The melody and lyrics are included in the book so that you can sing or simply follow along.

INCLUDES TAB

VOL. 1 – ROCK	00699570 / $16.99	
VOL. 2 – ACOUSTIC	00699569 / $16.95	
VOL. 3 – HARD ROCK	00699573 / $16.95	
VOL. 4 – POP/ROCK	00699571 / $16.99	
VOL. 5 – MODERN ROCK	00699574 / $16.99	
VOL. 6 – '90S ROCK	00699572 / $16.99	
VOL. 7 – BLUES	00699575 / $16.95	
VOL. 8 – ROCK	00699585 / $14.99	
VOL. 10 – ACOUSTIC	00699586 / $16.95	
VOL. 11 – EARLY ROCK	00699579 / $14.95	
VOL. 12 – POP/ROCK	00699587 / $14.95	
VOL. 13 – FOLK ROCK	00699581 / $15.99	
VOL. 14 – BLUES ROCK	00699582 / $16.95	
VOL. 15 – R&B	00699583 / $16.99	
VOL. 16 – JAZZ	00699584 / $15.95	
VOL. 17 – COUNTRY	00699588 / $15.95	
VOL. 18 – ACOUSTIC ROCK	00699577 / $15.95	
VOL. 19 – SOUL	00699578 / $14.99	
VOL. 20 – ROCKABILLY	00699580 / $14.95	
VOL. 21 – YULETIDE	00699602 / $14.95	
VOL. 22 – CHRISTMAS	00699600 / $15.95	
VOL. 23 – SURF	00699635 / $14.95	
VOL. 24 – ERIC CLAPTON	00699649 / $17.99	
VOL. 25 – LENNON & MCCARTNEY	00699642 / $16.99	
VOL. 26 – ELVIS PRESLEY	00699643 / $14.95	
VOL. 27 – DAVID LEE ROTH	00699645 / $16.95	
VOL. 28 – GREG KOCH	00699646 / $14.95	
VOL. 29 – BOB SEGER	00699647 / $15.99	
VOL. 30 – KISS	00699644 / $16.99	
VOL. 31 – CHRISTMAS HITS	00699652 / $14.95	
VOL. 32 – THE OFFSPRING	00699653 / $14.95	
VOL. 33 – ACOUSTIC CLASSICS	00699656 / $16.95	
VOL. 34 – CLASSIC ROCK	00699658 / $16.95	
VOL. 35 – HAIR METAL	00699660 / $16.95	
VOL. 36 – SOUTHERN ROCK	00699661 / $16.95	
VOL. 37 – ACOUSTIC UNPLUGGED	00699662 / $22.99	
VOL. 38 – BLUES	00699663 / $16.95	
VOL. 39 – '80S METAL	00699664 / $16.99	
VOL. 40 – INCUBUS	00699668 / $17.95	
VOL. 41 – ERIC CLAPTON	00699669 / $16.95	
VOL. 42 – 2000S ROCK	00699670 / $16.99	
VOL. 43 – LYNYRD SKYNYRD	00699681 / $17.95	
VOL. 44 – JAZZ	00699689 / $14.99	
VOL. 45 – TV THEMES	00699718 / $14.95	
VOL. 46 – MAINSTREAM ROCK	00699722 / $16.95	
VOL. 47 – HENDRIX SMASH HITS	00699723 / $19.95	
VOL. 48 – AEROSMITH CLASSICS	00699724 / $17.99	
VOL. 49 – STEVIE RAY VAUGHAN	00699725 / $17.99	
VOL. 50 – VAN HALEN 1978-1984	00110269 / $17.99	
VOL. 51 – ALTERNATIVE '90S	00699727 / $14.99	
VOL. 52 – FUNK	00699728 / $14.95	
VOL. 53 – DISCO	00699729 / $14.99	
VOL. 54 – HEAVY METAL	00699730 / $14.95	
VOL. 55 – POP METAL	00699731 / $14.95	
VOL. 56 – FOO FIGHTERS	00699749 / $15.99	
VOL. 58 – BLINK-182	00699772 / $14.95	
VOL. 59 – CHET ATKINS	00702347 / $16.99	
VOL. 60 – 3 DOORS DOWN	00699774 / $14.95	
VOL. 61 – SLIPKNOT	00699775 / $16.99	
VOL. 62 – CHRISTMAS CAROLS	00699798 / $12.95	
VOL. 63 – CREEDENCE CLEARWATER REVIVAL	00699802 / $16.99	

VOL. 64 – THE ULTIMATE OZZY OSBOURNE	00699803 / $16.99	
VOL. 66 – THE ROLLING STONES	00699807 / $16.95	
VOL. 67 – BLACK SABBATH	00699808 / $16.99	
VOL. 68 – PINK FLOYD – DARK SIDE OF THE MOON	00699809 / $16.99	
VOL. 69 – ACOUSTIC FAVORITES	00699810 / $14.95	
VOL. 70 – OZZY OSBOURNE	00699805 / $16.99	
VOL. 71 – CHRISTIAN ROCK	00699824 / $14.95	
VOL. 73 – BLUESY ROCK	00699829 / $16.99	
VOL. 75 – TOM PETTY	00699882 / $16.99	
VOL. 76 – COUNTRY HITS	00699884 / $14.95	
VOL. 77 – BLUEGRASS	00699910 / $14.99	
VOL. 78 – NIRVANA	00700132 / $16.99	
VOL. 79 – NEIL YOUNG	00700133 / $24.99	
VOL. 80 – ACOUSTIC ANTHOLOGY	00700175 / $19.95	
VOL. 81 – ROCK ANTHOLOGY	00700176 / $22.99	
VOL. 82 – EASY SONGS	00700177 / $12.99	
VOL. 83 – THREE CHORD SONGS	00700178 / $16.99	
VOL. 84 – STEELY DAN	00700200 / $16.99	
VOL. 85 – THE POLICE	00700269 / $16.99	
VOL. 86 – BOSTON	00700465 / $16.99	
VOL. 87 – ACOUSTIC WOMEN	00700763 / $14.99	
VOL. 88 – GRUNGE	00700467 / $16.99	
VOL. 89 – REGGAE	00700468 / $15.99	
VOL. 90 – CLASSICAL POP	00700469 / $14.99	
VOL. 91 – BLUES INSTRUMENTALS	00700505 / $14.99	
VOL. 92 – EARLY ROCK INSTRUMENTALS	00700506 / $14.99	
VOL. 93 – ROCK INSTRUMENTALS	00700507 / $16.99	
VOL. 94 – SLOW BLUES	00700508 / $16.99	
VOL. 95 – BLUES CLASSICS	00700509 / $14.99	
VOL. 96 – THIRD DAY	00700560 / $14.95	
VOL. 97 – ROCK BAND	00700703 / $14.99	
VOL. 99 – ZZ TOP	00700762 / $16.99	
VOL. 100 – B.B. KING	00700466 / $16.99	
VOL. 101 – SONGS FOR BEGINNERS	00701917 / $14.99	
VOL. 102 – CLASSIC PUNK	00700769 / $14.99	
VOL. 103 – SWITCHFOOT	00700773 / $16.99	
VOL. 104 – DUANE ALLMAN	00700846 / $16.99	
VOL. 105 – LATIN	00700939 / $16.99	
VOL. 106 – WEEZER	00700958 / $14.99	
VOL. 107 – CREAM	00701069 / $16.99	
VOL. 108 – THE WHO	00701053 / $16.99	
VOL. 109 – STEVE MILLER	00701054 / $14.99	
VOL. 110 – SLIDE GUITAR HITS	00701055 / $16.99	
VOL. 111 – JOHN MELLENCAMP	00701056 / $14.99	
VOL. 112 – QUEEN	00701052 / $16.99	
VOL. 113 – JIM CROCE	00701058 / $15.99	
VOL. 114 – BON JOVI	00701060 / $14.99	
VOL. 115 – JOHNNY CASH	00701070 / $16.99	
VOL. 116 – THE VENTURES	00701124 / $14.99	
VOL. 117 – BRAD PAISLEY	00701224 / $16.99	
VOL. 118 – ERIC JOHNSON	00701353 / $16.99	
VOL. 119 – AC/DC CLASSICS	00701356 / $17.99	
VOL. 120 – PROGRESSIVE ROCK	00701457 / $14.99	
VOL. 121 – U2	00701508 / $16.99	
VOL. 122 – CROSBY, STILLS & NASH	00701610 / $16.99	
VOL. 123 – LENNON & MCCARTNEY ACOUSTIC	00701614 / $16.99	
VOL. 125 – JEFF BECK	00701687 / $16.99	
VOL. 126 – BOB MARLEY	00701701 / $16.99	
VOL. 127 – 1970S ROCK	00701739 / $14.99	
VOL. 128 – 1960S ROCK	00701740 / $14.99	

VOL. 129 – MEGADETH	00701741 / $16.99	
VOL. 131 – 1990S ROCK	00701743 / $14.99	
VOL. 132 – COUNTRY ROCK	00701757 / $15.99	
VOL. 133 – TAYLOR SWIFT	00701894 / $16.99	
VOL. 134 – AVENGED SEVENFOLD	00701906 / $16.99	
VOL. 136 – GUITAR THEMES	00701922 / $14.99	
VOL. 137 – IRISH TUNES	00701966 / $15.99	
VOL. 138 – BLUEGRASS CLASSICS	00701967 / $14.99	
VOL. 139 – GARY MOORE	00702370 / $16.99	
VOL. 140 – MORE STEVIE RAY VAUGHAN	00702396 / $17.99	
VOL. 141 – ACOUSTIC HITS	00702401 / $16.99	
VOL. 143 – SLASH	00702425 / $19.99	
VOL. 144 – DJANGO REINHARDT	00702531 / $16.99	
VOL. 145 – DEF LEPPARD	00702532 / $16.99	
VOL. 146 – ROBERT JOHNSON	00702533 / $16.99	
VOL. 147 – SIMON & GARFUNKEL	14041591 / $16.99	
VOL. 148 – BOB DYLAN	14041592 / $16.99	
VOL. 149 – AC/DC HITS	14041593 / $17.99	
VOL. 150 – ZAKK WYLDE	02501717 / $16.99	
VOL. 152 – JOE BONAMASSA	02501751 / $19.99	
VOL. 153 – RED HOT CHILI PEPPERS	00702990 / $19.99	
VOL. 155 – ERIC CLAPTON – FROM THE ALBUM UNPLUGGED	00703085 / $16.99	
VOL. 156 – SLAYER	00703770 / $17.99	
VOL. 157 – FLEETWOOD MAC	00101382 / $16.99	
VOL. 158 – ULTIMATE CHRISTMAS	00101889 / $14.99	
VOL. 159 – WES MONTGOMERY	00102593 / $19.99	
VOL. 160 – T-BONE WALKER	00102641 / $16.99	
VOL. 161 – THE EAGLES – ACOUSTIC	00102659 / $17.99	
VOL. 162 – THE EAGLES HITS	00102667 / $17.99	
VOL. 163 – PANTERA	00103036 / $17.99	
VOL. 164 – VAN HALEN 1986-1995	00110270 / $17.99	
VOL. 166 – MODERN BLUES	00700764 / $16.99	
VOL. 167 – DREAM THEATER	00111938 / $24.99	
VOL. 168 – KISS	00113421 / $16.99	
VOL. 169 – TAYLOR SWIFT	00115982 / $16.99	
VOL. 170 – THREE DAYS GRACE	00117337 / $16.99	
VOL. 171 – JAMES BROWN	00117420 / $16.99	
VOL. 172 – THE DOOBIE BROTHERS	00119670 / $16.99	
VOL. 174 – SCORPIONS	00122119 / $16.99	
VOL. 175 – MICHAEL SCHENKER	00122127 / $16.99	
VOL. 176 – BLUES BREAKERS WITH JOHN MAYALL & ERIC CLAPTON	00122132 / $19.99	
VOL. 177 – ALBERT KING	00123271 / $16.99	
VOL. 178 – JASON MRAZ	00124165 / $17.99	
VOL. 179 – RAMONES	00127073 / $16.99	
VOL. 180 – BRUNO MARS	00129706 / $16.99	
VOL. 181 – JACK JOHNSON	00129854 / $16.99	
VOL. 182 – SOUNDGARDEN	00138161 / $17.99	
VOL. 184 – KENNY WAYNE SHEPHERD	00138258 / $17.99	
VOL. 185 – JOE SATRIANI	00139457 / $17.99	
VOL. 186 – GRATEFUL DEAD	00139459 / $17.99	
VOL. 187 – JOHN DENVER	00140839 / $17.99	
VOL. 189 – JOHN MAYER	00144350 / $17.99	

Complete song lists available online.

Prices, contents, and availability subject to change without notice.

HAL•LEONARD® CORPORATION

7777 W. BLUEMOUND RD. P.O. BOX 13819 MILWAUKEE, WI 53213
www.halleonard.com

0416